COPS, KILLERS AND STAYING ALIVE

The Murder of Police Officers in America

By

SAMUEL G. CHAPMAN

Professor, University of Oklahoma
Norman, Oklahoma

With a Foreword by

Jack E. Whitehouse, Ph.D.

Dean, Southern State University
Huntington Beach, California

CHARLES C THOMAS • PUBLISHER
Springfield • Illinois • U.S.A.

Published and Distributed Throughout the World by

CHARLES C THOMAS • PUBLISHER

2600 South First Street

Springfield, Illinois 62708-4709

© *1986 by* CHARLES C THOMAS • PUBLISHER

ISBN 0-398-05222-0

Library of Congress Catalog Card Number: 85-31825

With **THOMAS BOOKS** *careful attention is given to all details of manufacturing and
design. It is the Publisher's desire to present books that are satisfactory as to their physical
qualities and artistic possibilities and appropriate for their particular use.* THOMAS
BOOKS *will be true to those laws of quality that assure a good name and good will.*

Printed in the United States of America
Q-R-3

Library of Congress Cataloging in Publication Data

Chapman, Samuel G.
    Cops, killers, and staying alive.

    Bibliography: p.
    Includes index.
    1. Police murders—United States. 2. Police mur-
ders—Oklahoma. 3. Police murders—United States—
Prevention. I. Title.
HV8138.C52 1986   364.1'523'0883632   85-31825
ISBN 0-398-05222-0

FOREWORD

THE POLICEMAN holds an ambivalent place in the hearts and minds of many Americans. When a citizen receives a traffic citation or is told of his child's malicious behavior, an officer may be perceived as a villain. Conversely, when a police officer recovers your child's stolen bicycle or renders life saving aid at the scene of an auto accident he becomes a respected hero.

Few people are aware of the compilation of circumstances and factors that lead to a police death. Yet when there is a fatality, a unique phenomenon occurs. Initially, the victim assumes a kind of sainthood. Then there are services which often resemble a happening, one which features political and civic figures, flowers galore, scores of police officers, and emotion of a high order. There is also a bereaved widow, dressed in subdued colors, and the dead officer's parents. Also prominent are his partners, holding the toddlers, and a statuelike uniformed lawman playing Taps while shots are fired over the flag-draped coffin. This is the stereotypical funeral afforded police.

While no other occupational group in America has a higher prospect of being murdered than law enforcement officers, it is strikingly apparent that only a handful of specialists have researched and analyzed the total phenomenon of police homicides. Perhaps the foremost authority is Professor Samuel G. Chapman, whose book, **Cops, Killers and Staying Alive: The Murder of Police Officers in America**, will go a long way toward redressing this glaring information gap.

This publication is neither a simplistic, narrow approach to the subject of police murders, nor intended to compete with those books which address merely street survival techniques. It, in contrast to all others, offers a broadly based approach to addressing a wide variety of issues in order to reduce the number of police assaults and deaths which occur every year.

While Professor Chapman's book sets out excellent advice about how to stay alive on the street, most importantly, he takes his readership well beyond such a narrow focus and discusses what other institutions, communities, bodies, and individuals should be doing to protect the street officer. For example, legislative bodies can enact certain laws which would enhance police officer safety just as the rash of kidnappings for ransom, which occurred in the 1930s, were brought to a standstill nationwide when the death penalty was enacted as a punishment for kidnappings. City managers, police administrators, training directors, mayors, researchers, citizen's groups, and others have an important part to play in the effort to reduce police homicides, too.

Cops, Killers and Staying Alive has been written by one of the best minds in the American criminal justice field. The superior quality of this book reflects the fact that Professor Chapman is not just another academic dilettante. He is a realist with significant experience in the real world during his 35 rich years of professional life. Before his professorships at Michigan State University and the University of Oklahoma, Chapman had several years police street experience with the Berkeley Police Department in California and was chief of police of the Multnomah County, Oregon, Sheriff's Department in Portland. His work as assistant director of the President's Crime Commission has been widely heralded as invaluable. For years, his knowledge and expertise have been in demand nationally as an expert witness on police procedures. Professor Chapman has extensive experience in the real world political arena, too, having served for eleven years as an elected member of the city council and vice-mayor of Norman, Oklahoma. He has also travelled worldwide to extend the benefit of his knowledge and expertise in law enforcement administration to U.S. military personnel, having taught in Panama, Japan, Korea, Guam, Okinawa, Spain, and Germany.

As a frequent and significant contributor to the professional literature, Chapman's numerous publications are always well received. In fact, references to his work are found in many of the important texts in law enforcement. In 1973-74 he was director of the exhaustive **Police Assaults Study**, which established him as one of the leading experts on police murders and assaults.

Clearly, there is no other book like this one. It is a product of Professor Chapman's police experience, political acumen, and education. After analyzing police officer murders, he sets out unique and innovative countermeasures which, when implemented, should reduce police casualties. No other book does this.

This outstanding book is timely, overdue, concise (thank you, Lord), and inspiring. Chapman analyzes what has happened in the past and what can, should, and must be done to avoid these events from occurring again, and again, in the future. As always with Professor Chapman's writings, this work is highly readable, with a blessed absence of academic jargon and obscure words and phrases. Refreshingly, Professor Chapman writes for the working professional, not other academicians.

Without doubt, **Cops, Killers and Staying Alive** should be afforded a prominent place in libraries the free world over.

Jack Edward Whitehouse, Ph.D.
Dean
School of Behavioral Science
Southern States University
Huntington Beach, California

PREFACE

THIS BOOK began to take form in 1951 in Berkeley, California, where I patrolled as a street cop, working nights while going to graduate school at the University of California each day. Like other officers, I had my share of serious scrapes and on several occasions narrowly missed being seriously injured or killed. In the 1960s, as police chief of the 250-member Multnomah County Sheriff's Police Department in Portland, Oregon, accounts of attacks on officers crossed my desk, and the urgent need of research and analysis concerning police deaths and the reduction of risks became apparent. In 1972, while teaching police science at the University of Oklahoma, I assumed yet another role — that of an elected member of the Norman City Council, where I served for eleven years. While in that role, one of the city's young officers was murdered as he and others attempted to apprehend a felon, yet again underscoring the vast need for this study.

This book, then, is a synthesis of my personal experiences as a street cop, and my concern for officer safety that took shape while I served as a police administrator, university professor, and a local political figure. Its content sets forth ideas about what street cops, trainers, police administrators, city managers, legislators, and researchers can do to reduce assaults on police, even though they are in highly diverse roles.

There are some things this book **isn't**. It's not another book on street survival, exhorting officers to duck when the shots ring out. It isn't a book of quick fixes to the assaults problem, either, for there are no sure-fire ways to prevent attacks on police. And it is not a book of light reading, as its content challenges people in varied sectors to thoughtfully act on proposals which range from training, to legislation, to research.

There are some things this book **is**. It's a book dedicated to life, and life-saving. It says let's do more, much more, than merely wringing our hands and burying our dead in the wake of each officer murder! Let's insist that action be taken on many fronts to reduce police casualties. It's a book which calls for breaking the myopic view that casualty reduction is only a matter of street tactics. And it's a book which frankly states that one of every two officers is the principal contributor to his own demise through his carelessness or complacency. If only we could reduce officer carelessness and complacency, we'll have made monumental strides in helping officers help themselves to stay alive!

Several organizations and people have been instrumental in bringing this book to fruition. These include the Federal Bureau of Investigation and the Law Enforcement Assistance Administration. Several agencies of Oklahoma state government played important roles, too. These include the Department of Corrections; the State Bureau of Investigation; the Office of the State Medical Examiner; the State Health Department; the Oklahoma Highway Patrol; and the Council on Law Enforcement Education and Training.

Dozens of people helped move this research ahead. Among these are: Chiefs Don Holyfield and Ed Smith of, respectively, the Norman and Chickasha Police Departments; Captains Mike Lapuzza and Jerry Cook of the Oklahoma Highway Patrol; The Honorable Alan J. Couch, Associate District Judge, Cleveland County, Oklahoma; and Dan Holman, Ricky Wayne Cink, Steve Presson, and Patti Poole, students within the University of Oklahoma's Law Enforcement Administration program. Jean Hofvendahl of Oakland, California, provided valuable editorial assistance and encouragement.

Chief Dan Hollingsworth, Oklahoma City Police Department, retired, deserves specific notice. Hollingsworth, as a consultant to the Oklahoma Highway Patrol's Training Center, has put together a Living Textbook series of in-service training programs which feature newspaper articles clipped from dailys nationwide. The Living Textbook series was central to the preparation of **Cops, Killers and Staying Alive**.

The book was indexed by one of my colleagues, Jeanne G. Howard, Assistant Professor of Bibliography at the University of Oklahoma.

Clerical assistance was crucial, too. Six staff members of the University of Oklahoma's Information Processing Center were stalwart performers: Mary McClain; Donna Epperson; Debi DeSilver; Pamela Henne; Susan Houck; and Debbie Rettig. Three members of the Department of Political Science support staff were key to this production, too. The remarkable patience, perseverence and clerical skills of Geri Rowden, Beverly Sue Webb Whitecrow, and Mary Slepka are gratefully recognized.

Finally, three persons warrant special recognition for having kept this enterprise moving ahead with cohesion, discipline, and in accord with a deadline. These are Ann Geiger, former student and now an attorney-at-law in Oklahoma City; Professor Dale Bay, former graduate student and faculty member at the Naval Academy of South Korea; and Dr. Jack E. Whitehouse, Dean, School of Behavioral Science, Southern States University, Huntington Beach, California, and former Culver City, California, police officer. These three persons were constructive critics, editors, trouble shooters, advisors on form and layout, and all-round performers.

Now a few words about gender. I hope no one will be offended by my use of gender-specific terms and pronouns in this book. The fact that I have opted to use the standard "he-him-his-lawman" form by no means implies that I am insensitive to females nor that I am denigrating women in any way. On the contrary, I am keenly aware of the increasing numbers of women who are serving in police roles and who, like their male counterparts, are victims of attacks. I have chosen to use the traditional masculine terms merely in the interest of readability.

I've paid special attention to the preparation of the tables. I cannot vouch for the accuracy of the national sets of data, for I had no dominion over their original classification or compilation. Whatever inconsistencies may surface in other-than-the-Oklahoma data must be acknowledged as the product of persons other than myself.

In conclusion, while many helped in the book's preparation, I accept full responsibility for its virtues or limitations. My hope is that **Cops, Killers and Staying Alive** will serve as a wellspring of ideas and supermarket of concepts which a host of people and organizations will draw upon to make police officers everywhere safer.

Samuel G. Chapman

INTRODUCTION

ABOUT July 1, 1985, the one-millionth assault on an American police officer happened since records were first kept, starting in 1960. The attacks resulted in the murder of 2,129 police and the injury of about 328,000 others. There were some 631,000 incidents where lawmen suffered no injury other than the humiliation of an attack on themselves.

What makes with these figures? How did things get this way? What are the stories behind the Big Story? And, importantly, what can be done about this problem?

This book is dedicated to the reduction of police casualties.

Nationally, the incidence of police deaths has grown notably since 1960, when the FBI first published annual data which highlighted this type of murder. With little relief, that number became greater each year to a high of 132 victims in 1974. While fewer lawmen have been murdered each year since then, there have still been significantly more than the 28 who fell in 1960.

With only one significant exception between 1972-1975, assaults on police officers have, like deaths, shown an almost consistent increase over the 9,621 attacks reported by the FBI in 1960. The number of police officers assaulted and murdered each year from 1960 through 1984 is shown in Table 1.

The FBI publishes a major report each year, as well as a summary each quarter, which sets out the dimensions of crime in the United States. Called **Uniform Crime Reports: Crime in the United States**, the Bureau publication features seven Index Offenses, those classes of crime shown by experience to be most generally and completely reported to the police. An eighth Index Offense, arson, was reported starting in 1978.

Each year since 1960, the **Uniform Crime Report** has included a narrative and tables about assaults on police and their murder, too. Starting with 1972, the Bureau has supplemented its **Uniform Crime**

Report each year with a companion publication called **Law Enforcement Officers Killed and Assaulted**, which provides comprehensive statistical data regarding police killings and assaults, but little analysis.

Table 1

THE NUMBER OF ASSAULTS ON POLICE OFFICERS AND POLICE OFFICERS MURDERED BY YEAR 1960 THROUGH 1984

Year	Total Assaults	Rate Per 100 Officers	Assaults with Injury	Rate Per 100 Officers	Number Of Police Officers Murdered	Officer Deaths Owing To Accidents
1960	9,621	6.3	NR*	NR	28	20
1961	13,190	8.3	NR	NR	37	34
1962	17,330	10.2	NR	NR	48	30
1963	16,793	11.0	NR	NR	55	33
1964	18,001	9.9	7,738	4.3	57	31
1965	20,523	10.8	6,836	3.6	53	30
1966	23,851	12.2	9,113	4.6	57	42
1967	26,755	13.5	10,770	5.4	76	47
1968	33,604	15.8	14,072	6.6	64	59
1969	35,202	16.9	11,949	5.7	86	39
1970	43,171	18.7	15,165	6.6	100	46
1971	49,768	18.7	17,631	6.6	126	52
1972	37,523	15.1	12,230	5.8	112	41
1973	32,535	15.0	12,880	5.9	127	40
1974	29,511	15.1	11,468	5.9	132	47
1975	44,867	15.4	18,974	6.5	129	56
1976	49,079	16.8	18,737	6.4	111	29
1977	49,156	15.3	17,663	5.5	93	32
1978	56,130	16.1	21,075	6.2	93	52
1979	59,031	17.3	21,764	6.4	106	58
1980	57,847	16.7	21,516	6.2	104	61
1981	57,116	17.2	20,272	6.1	91	66
1982	55,755	17.5	17,116	5.4	92	72
1983	62,324	16.5	20,807	5.5	80	72
1984	60,153	16.2	20,205	5.4	72	75

Source: Federal Bureau of Investigation, *Uniform Crime Reports* (Washington, D.C.: U.S. Government Printing Office). Data were extracted from each *Uniform Crime Report* for the years set out above.

*NR: Not reported in *Uniform Crime Reports* until 1964.

The column farthest to the right in Table 1 is included merely for the record. It sets out, by year since 1960, the number of police nationally who have lost their lives through accidents, not murder incidents. These include deaths stemming from motor vehicle, motorcycle or aircraft crashes, falls, drownings, etc. These numbers, like the data pertaining to murder incidents, have been derived from annual reports prepared by the FBI.

One portion of Table 1 warrants clarification, since the figures could be highly misleading unless the reader knows what prompted some dramatics. Note that in 1971, there were about five times the number of officers assaulted as were victimized in 1960. Was it really about five times more dangerous to be an officer in 1971 than eleven years earlier? Not at all: it merely reflects that fact that with any new program, participants take a while to get into the swing of things. Reporting became more widespread as years passed.

Then, all of a sudden with the 1972 assaults figures, it becomes "safer" to be a police officer, and dramatically so, in contrast to 1971. It is even more so for 1973 and 1974. Then, quick as a wink, 1975 brings about a sharp reversal of the downward trend: it's no longer "safer" to be an officer. Then the numbers are, generally, up through 1984.

It wasn't actually "safer" to be a police officer from 1972-74 than in 1971, even though the data infer that conclusion. Rather, the numerical plunge is explained by a failure of many forces to report attacks on officers to the FBI for these years. For example, in 1971, 21 forces across the nation serving cities of from 100,000 to 750,000 population failed to report assaults to the FBI. In 1972, 69 forces serving these size cities provided no assault data at all! This reporting gap characterized the numbers for 1973 and 1974, too.

The underreporting for 1972-74 may be traced to a major revision in the form on which forces were asked by the FBI to report assaults on officers. From 1960 through 1971, the form used by the FBI to collect these data was very easy to execute. Shown as Form One, it included but three entries. Since January 1, 1972, however, the annual report form was substantially revised as the FBI sought to assemble a more complete set of assault-related information. The new form, shown as Form Two, had some **175** boxes to complete. The task proved too much for many forces. Hence the misleadingly modest numbers of 1972-74. Police statisticians became more comfortable with the form as time passed. By 1975, more representative numbers were the result.

While the numbers of officers assaulted each year are underreported, the FBI's figures on officers murdered are an accurate accounting. Details about the incidents, the victims, the suspects, and what happened to people who murder police are important to determine. It is crucial to spell out measures which, when implemented, can prevent officers from becoming casualties.

Throughout Part I of this book, frequent reference is made to two sets of data. The first set is information derived from an in-depth analysis of 52 incidents from January 1, 1950, through December 31, 1984, in which 54 Oklahoma police officers were murdered on duty. An incredible amount of information about these cases was compiled from a list of sources, including the forces for which the victims worked, the Oklahoma State Bureau of Investigation, the FBI, court records and trial transcripts, the Office of the State Medical Examiner, death certificates and autopsy reports, the Oklahoma Department of Corrections, and the State Historical Society. In addition, newspaper accounts were helpful in filling in data gaps, as were interviews with victims' families, prosecutors, defense counsel, veteran lawmen, witnesses, trial judges, and so forth. These sources and others provided the threads from which the complicated social and technical tapestry of each incident could be woven together. Only by so doing could there be the analysis of all interlocking elements of each murder.

The second data set is information derived from the FBI's **Uniform Crime Reports** and **Law Enforcement Officers Killed and Assaulted**.

The countermeasures, which are the centerpiece of Part II of this book, have been put together from an analysis of the Oklahoma and national pictures spelled out in Part I.

To summarize, then, the increasing numbers of both fatal and nonfatal attacks on officers has prompted concern about the occupational safety of police, not just from among the officers themselves but from quarters outside law enforcement. In fact, murders and assaults on police officers lessen the appeal of law enforcement as a career, polarize the public, and jeopardize the American concept of liberty within the framework of law. Clearly, a critical problem exists nationwide, and some means must be found to reduce assaults on police officers and the murders which stem from such victimization.

FORM ONE

R-76 (Rev. 9-4-67)   Bureau Budget No. 43-R005.9

NUMBER OF FULL-TIME LAW ENFORCEMENT EMPLOYEES AS OF DECEMBER 31, 1967
NUMBER OF OFFICERS KILLED AND ASSAULTED

City _____

County _____

State _____

This form is to be used to report all full-time employees on the payroll of your law enforcement agency as of December 31, 1967. Your figures should show all law enforcement officers (sworn personnel) opposite item 1, and full-time civilian employees opposite item 2. The total of items 1 and 2 should be placed opposite item 3.

Items and Instructions

1. Full-time law enforcement officers *(Include Chief, Sheriff, Commissioner, Superintendent)* .... _____
   Include only full-time law enforcement officers on your agency's payroll as of December 31 who work your usual full-time workweek. Do not count special officers, merchant police or others who are not paid with law enforcement funds.

2. Full-time civilian employees *(Do not count school crossing guards)*. . _____
   Include only full-time civilian employees of your department who worked full-time during December (clerks, stenographers, mechanics, etc., who do not have police powers). Count them if they are on leave with pay. If they are not paid from police funds do not count them.

3. Total full-time law enforcement officers and civilian employees .... _____
   (Total of items 1 and 2)

OFFICERS KILLED - Number of full-time law enforcement officers belonging to your organization who were killed in line of duty during the year _____

OFFICERS ASSAULTED - Number of full-time law enforcement officers belonging to your organization who were assaulted in line of duty during the year resulting in:

Injury to employee _____

No injury _____

Do Not Write Here	
Recorded	_____
Reviewed	_____
Punched	_____
Verified	_____

_____   _____   _____
Date   Prepared By   Title

_____
Chief, Sheriff, Commissioner, Superintendent

Please forward this form by January 22 to: **Director, Federal Bureau of Investigation, Washington, D. C. 20535**

FORM TWO

12-106 (Rev. 4-18-72)   Bureau Budget No. 43-R0 500

LAW ENFORCEMENT OFFICERS KILLED OR ASSAULTED

It is requested this report be completed and transmitted with monthly crime reports to: Director, Federal Bureau of Investigation, Uniform Crime Reports, Washington, D. C. 20535. This form should be used to report the number of your officers who were assaulted or killed in the line of duty during the month. Additional information concerning officers killed will be requested by a separate questionnaire.

OFFICERS KILLED
Number of your law enforcement officers | By felonious act _____
killed in the line of duty this month. | By accident or negligence _____

Officers Assaulted (Do not include officers killed) - See other side for instructions.

Type of Activity	Total Assaults by Weapon A	Type of Weapon				Type of Assignment							Police Assaults Cleared M
		Firearm B	Knife or Other Cutting Instrument C	Other Dangerous Weapon D	Hands, Fists, Feet, etc. E	Two-Man Vehicle F	One-Man Vehicle		Detective or Special Assign.		Other		
							Alone G	Assisted H	Alone I	Assisted J	Alone K	Assisted L	
1. Responding to "Disturbance" calls (family quarrels, man with gun, etc.)													
2. Burglaries in progress or pursuing burglary suspects													
3. Robberies in progress or pursuing robbery suspects													
4. Attempting other arrests													
5. Civil disorder (riot, mass disobedience)													
6. Handling, transporting, custody of prisoners. . .													
7. Investigating suspicious persons or circumstances													
8. Ambush - no warning . .													
9. Mentally deranged													
10. Traffic pursuits and stops.													
11. All other													
12. TOTAL (1-11)													
13. Number with personal injury . .													
14. Number without personal injury .													
15. Time of assaults . . . . AM PM													

12:01   2:00   4:00   6:00   8:00   10:00   12:00

DO NOT WRITE HERE

	Initials
Recorded	
Edited	
Punched	
Verified	
Adjusted	

_____   _____   _____   _____
Month and Year   Agency Identifier   Prepared by   Title

_____   _____   _____
Agency   State   Chief, Sheriff, Commissioner, Superintendent

FORM TWO (CONTINUED)

INSTRUCTIONS FOR PREPARING REPORT

When an officer is assaulted in the line of duty, an entry should be made on the appropriate line for type of activity (lines 1-11), under type of weapons used (columns B-E), and under type of assignment (columns F-L). An entry should also be made in either line 13 (injury) or line 14 (no injury). Also count the assault by the time of day on line 15.

When any of these assaults are cleared, an entry should be made under column M for appropriate activity.

At the end of the month, add all lines under columns B through E and enter in column A. The total of columns F through L should equal the total of columns B through E as entered in column A. Also add all columns down and enter in line 12.

Columns B-E:

If more than one type of weapon is used to commit a single assault, the column encountered moving from left to right (B to E) which shows one of the weapons used should be selected for the entry. Do not enter any of the other different types of weapons which were used.

Columns F-L:

Column F (Two-Man Vehicle) and columns G and H (One-Man Vehicle) pertain to uniformed officers; columns I and J (Detective or Special Assignment) to non-uniformed officers; columns K and L (Other) to officers assaulted while in a capacity not represented by columns F-J such as foot patrol, off duty, etc.

Column M:

In column M count the number of "assault on officer" offenses cleared. Do not count the number of persons arrested for such offenses. Include exceptional clearances.

Lines 1-11:

Indicate the type of police activity the officer was engaged in at the time he was assaulted.

Line 12:

Enter the total of lines 1-11.

Line 13:

Enter the number of assaults from line 12 which resulted in personal injury to the officer.

Line 14:

Enter the number of assaults from line 12 in which there was no injury to the officer.

Line 15:

Enter the total number of assaults on police officers occurring within the appropriate two-hour intervals.

CONTENTS

LIST OF TABLES

COPS, KILLERS AND
STAYING ALIVE

PART I

THE INCIDENT, ACTORS,
AND DISPOSITION

COP FIGHTING across America is a national disgrace and must be dealt with. A logical beginning is to assemble information about the incidents which led to police murders. Then we must determine who the victims and suspects are. After that, we must determine what happens to cop killers in our criminal justice system. After analyzing these elements, countermeasures may be identified which promise to reduce the carnage among cops.

CHAPTER I

THE STAGE

BEFORE DETERMINING who is involved, it is important to assemble the facts of each incident in order to find out what happened. Identifying the anatomy of confrontation is a good beginning for a prescriptive package.

THE INCIDENT

It is evening, shortly before midnight. It is warm. Gunfire rings out, suddenly breaking the peaceful silence of this summer evening. An officer in uniform, helped by another member of the force, is attempting to make an arrest. One lawman is hit, mortally wounded in the body by slugs from a .38 calibre handgun. This was one of several different ways an officer lost his life in Oklahoma.

About 1:00 A.M., in a large Oklahoma city, a lone officer stopped a car for what appeared to be a routine traffic citation. The officer stepped from his car and ordered the three men out of theirs. The driver, rather than producing his driver's license, came up with a .25 calibre automatic from beneath his shirt and shot the officer three times in the chest and abdomen. As the three rushed back to their car to get away, the mortally wounded officer was heard to moan. One of the passengers went back to the officer, took the lawman's gun from its holster and coldly fired a fourth shot into the back of the officer's head. The suspects were arrested within two weeks. This is another way an officer met death.

The Chase

The chase starts at once, thanks to an early scent of trouble, when the trail is hottest. When finally confronted, the suspect may shoot it out with police. On the other hand, facing overwhelming numbers of police and the certainty of arrest, a suspect may take his life. Most suspects surrender meekly, hardly resembling the television-inspired image of macho cop killers.

Most apprehensions have been made within a few days, but occasionally it takes authorities up to a week to press the case, find the suspects, and make an arrest. Wondrously, it has been since the April 14, 1949, slaying of a Tulsa officer that a cop killer escaped detection in Oklahoma!

Actually, most chases were of short duration, for, of the 69 suspects in the 54 murders, 47 were cornered within 24 hours of the incident. Of these, 35 were arrested, eight were killed by police in shootouts immediately after an officer was murdered, and four committed suicide rather than submit to arrest. Of the other 22 suspects, 16 were arrested within a week of the slaying and five were arrested within two weeks. Only one suspect was at large for a longer period — 198 days. If these 198 days are excluded, the 57 suspects taken alive were apprehended within an average of but 1.5 days.

The state's perfect clearance rate in these 52 police-killing incidents over the 35-year span is a tribute to the skill, investigative tenacity, and ability of the state's lawmen and agencies to work well with each other. Oklahoma's perfect clearance rate, impressive by any standard, assumes greater significance in that the national clearance rate for police killings is about 93 percent since 1960.

How Often Does It Happen?

Whether urban or rural in setting, it happens. In Oklahoma, there was an average of one officer-murder incident every 246 days over the 35-year span. The data in Table 2 show the date of each incident and the interval by days from the last officer murder. Two dates — September 3, 1949, and May 8, 1985 — are included as the dates of murders immediately previous and subsequent to the 35-year span.

Of the incidents, there were 24 where the interval between them was greater than the 246-day average. The greatest interval was the 1,181-day span between a July, 1964, murder of an Oklahoma City officer and the October, 1967, slaying of a Washita County deputy sheriff. Remarkably, this extraordinary record was almost equalled by 1,177-day span, running from September, 1979, to December, 1982.

Of the 28 incidents where the interval between them was shorter than the 246-day average, there were only 30 minutes between the murders of two highway patrol troopers and the killing of a highway patrol lieutenant on Memorial Day weekend of 1978 in rural southern Oklahoma during a massive manhunt for two state penitentiary escapees. In 1974, two other incidents happened within about one hour of each other.

Table 2

THE INTERVAL, BY DAYS, FROM THE LAST PREVIOUS MURDER INCIDENT IN OKLAHOMA 1950-1984

Date	Days From Last Previous Murder	Date	Days From Last Previous Murder
6-30-50	300	6-28-70	320
*5-17-51	321	7-28-70	30
11-13-51	180	11-02-70	97
12-13-51	30	2-17-71	107
1-03-52	21	*4-02-71	44
6-26-53	540	*6-14-71	73
6-27-53	1	5-21-72	342
9-05-53	70	*7-30-72	70
*9-14-53	9	*9-18-72	50
6-12-54	271	5-02-73	226
7-11-54	29	*4-16-74	349
*7-16-54	5	7-25-74	100
*12-11-54	148	7-25-74	1 hour
7-04-56	571	6-29-75	339
5-20-57	320	*4-04-77	645
4-28-58	343	6-18-77	75
1-23-59	270	12-10-77	175
12-22-60	699	5-26-78	167
*4-26-62	490	5-26-78	30 minutes
5-20-62	24		
6-16-62	27	*9-01-78	98
2-03-63	232	*9-19-79	383
10-11-63	250	*12-09-82	1,177
*7-27-64	290	1-05-83	27
10-21-67	1,181	*10-05-83	273
7-30-68	283	10-27-84	388
8-12-69	378	(5-08-85	163)

*Officers murdered in urban settings, sixteen in all.

The two desperados who so coldly murdered the three highway patrol personnel were killed by police gunfire at the Caddo, Oklahoma site where the lieutenant was fatally hit by a .12 gauge shotgun slug. The person who murdered the two eastern Oklahoma lawmen within an hour was taken alive, tried, and convicted of both killings.

ACTIVITY PERFORMED WHEN MURDERED

Table 3 shows the types of activites in which officers were engaged when murdered. Unfortunately, the categories of activities have not been identified with consistency over the 25-year period that the FBI has published these figures. For example, for the first five years, the FBI lumped into one category: 1) persons murdered while transporting prisoners; 2) officers killed while attempting other arrests; and 3) those who were murdered while making apparently routine traffic stops. In addition, ambush and civil disorders deaths were not specifically categorized until 1965.

When one contrasts what the 54 Oklahoma victims were doing with what the 1,918 officers nationally were engaged in from 1965-1984, there is a remarkable percentage similarity between the two groups in seven of the eleven categories of activity. There are notable dissimilarities in three of the categories: 1) burglaries; 2) robberies in progress; and 3) handling prisoners.

Just why Oklahoma lawmen have had such good fortune in handling hot burglary and robbery calls, but such dismal luck in handling prisoners in contrast with police nationwide, is not known. It certainly is not because the state lacks burglars or robbers — the state's crime rate is hardly modest. At the same time, however, Oklahoma has a very high ratio of people in penal institutions, when compared with the national backdrop, which suggests high numbers of police-suspect confrontation, an inference which may be drawn from the fact that it is lawmen who initiate a person's trip to the penitentiary.

Responding to Disturbance Calls

Nine of 54 officers were gunned down while responding to disturbance calls. These deaths came during, but are not limited to, the traditionally very dangerous domestic fights. In seven of these instances, there were two or more officers present, while only two were alone. In one of these solo incidents, an officer in a very small town was murdered

Table 3

LAW ENFORCEMENT OFFICERS KILLED
BY TYPE OF ACTIVITY
1960-1984

Type of Activity	Oklahoma 1950-1984		Nationally 1960-1964		Nationally 1965-1984	
	Number	Percent	Number	Percent	Number	Percent
Responding to disturbance calls (family quarrels, man with gun, etc.)	9	16.7	45	20.0	310	16.2
Burglaries in progress or pursuing burglary suspects	2	3.7	28	12.4	121	6.3
Robberies in progress or pursuing robbery suspects	4	7.4	51	22.7	341	17.8
Attempting other arrests (excludes arrests for burglaries and robberies)	15	27.8	62	27.6	438	22.8
Civil disorders (mass disobedience, riot, etc.)	–	–	–	–	14	.7
Handling, transporting, custody of prisoners	6	11.1	–	–	82	4.3
Investigating suspicious persons or circumstances	6	11.1	28	12.4	168	8.7
Ambush (entrapment and premeditation)	3	5.6	–	–	95	5.0
Ambush (unprovoked attack)	1	1.8	–	–	73	3.8
Mentally deranged	1	1.8	11	4.9	58	3.0
Traffic pursuits and stops	7	13.0	–	–	218	11.4
TOTALS	54	100.0	225	100.0	1,918	100.0

by a man creating a scene because his son had been arrested earlier. In the second incident, an Ardmore assistant chief responded to a domestic spat involving two men and a woman — and was mistaken by one man as the other in the triangle! The chief was gunned down in a residence driveway on a January evening as he sought to determine what had prompted an earlier call for help from that home.

One case where the victim was assisted came during rodeo time in July. It was shortly after midnight when police got a call from a hotel clerk reporting the theft of a shotgun. There was a drunken suspect. Three officers and a merchant patrolman started up an outside stairway to come in from behind and thereby surprise the suspect, who was reported to be on the second floor. Obviously not surprised, the suspect suddenly leaped onto a second floor landing and fired, killing an officer. The suspect committed suicide before being captured.

Burglaries in Progress

Two of 54 Okalahoma officers were murdered while intervening during burglaries in progress. The percentage of officers so murdered is somewhat below the national picture, over a 25-year span. One of the Oklahoma deaths sounds like a rerun of a scene which has plagued police for decades and is one of the most typical of all the Oklahoma murders.

About 1:00A.M. on a cold Thursday morning on December 22, 1960, a grocery store watchman, alerted by noises, called police for assistance in checking the building. Officers in a two-man patrol unit responded. The three men surprised four suspects in the act of burglary. From outside the store, officers ordered the suspects to surrender and come out of the grocery. A pistol shot was fired from within the store, striking an officer in the chest, killing him instantly. One suspect was killed by return fire. Three other suspects fled and were arrested in Fort Worth, Texas a few days later. Christmas was bleak in Ardmore, for a popular 29-year old officer was dead. He left a wife and three small youngsters.

Robberies in Progress

That far fewer Oklahoma lawmen have lost their lives while intervening during hot robberies than officers nationally, may be partly explained by reviewing comparative robbery crime index rates. In 1984, the robbery index crime rate per 100,000 population for the nation as a whole was almost double the 111.2 rate in Oklahoma, a pattern which has been consistent year after year.

One of the robberies is particularly interesting and shows the chance aspect of some of these cases. It occurred in a cafe in a very small Oklahoma town. A deputy sheriff had stopped for supper and was in the process of exiting. A robber, not aware of the deputy's presence, was in the process of entering to hold up the place. The two came literally face-to-face, startling each other. The deputy was struck in the chest by one blast at close range from a .20 gauge shotgun.

Attempting Other Arrests

A Tulsa detective was assigned to help four federal agents execute a search warrant in a narcotics case. Upon reaching the house, the five men split up. The city detective and one federal agent covered the back while the other three agents knocked on the front door and charged inside. The agents who entered saw a man pull a .25 calibre pistol, and ducked just in time to miss being hit by a shot. The suspect dashed for the back door, yanked it open, and leaped outside. He missed another agent with a shot before he dropped the Tulsa detective sergeant with one shot in the heart. The suspect was arrested, charged, and convicted of murder.

This was what happened to one of the 15 officers murdered while attempting to make an arrest for other than robberies or burglaries in progress. In 11 of the 15 incidents, the victims were in the presence of at least one other officer and, in some cases, many others—as above. These incidents were characterized by the fact that the department had advance notice that a wanted suspect was at a particular location. Therefore, usually two or more personnel set out to make the arrest.

Transporting Prisoners

Six officers were murdered in five separate instances while transporting prisoners. In four of the cases, the suspect was **not** handcuffed, a prime contributing factor to the murder. There are no national data on the restraint/fatality issue.

One of the incidents where the suspect was not handcuffed centers around an arrest for a felony. An officer in a large metropolitan area went to a hotel to pick up a rape suspect already in the custody of other personnel. Carelessly, the suspect was neither searched nor handcuffed before the officer ordered the suspect to get into the back seat of the police car. On the way to headquarters, the unrestrained suspect grabbed the officer's clipboard and crashed it down on the lawman's head, causing the car to jump a curb. The officer tried to fight off the suspect, but the man had drawn a 7.65 Beretta pistol which had been concealed on his person and, of course, had not been found because no search had been made. The officer was shot in the right side, the bullet ripping into his heart. Death was instantaneous. The suspect was rearrested within minutes.

In yet another instance, two officers were transporting two felony suspects to the county jail. Their prisoners were handcuffed and placidly resting in the back seat. Suddenly, one reached over the front seat and grabbed the steering wheel, jerking it abruptly and causing the cruiser to cross into the opposing traffic lane. While the officers fought the prisoner, the car crashed headlong into an oncoming car. The officers were killed instantly; the two prisoners were not seriously injured.

The high incidence of murder while transporting prisoners may be linked to the geography of Oklahoma. There are hundreds of rural communities, many of which have no jail, or one which is old, substandard, and not safe. Also, distances are great, which maximizes officer exposure to attack when they must transport prisoners to detention centers in large cities or counties or to the state penitentiary at McAlester. Finally, the police must transport prisoners to state hospitals for purposes of sanity determination. Officers may tend to become lax when they make these kinds of runs regularly, failing to appreciate their extraordinary exposure on this kind of mission.

In summary, the failure to adequately search prisoners before transport, the failure to handcuff prisoners during transport, the absence of a device separating front from rear cabs, the repetitious nature of transport missions, and perhaps even boredom and fatigue inherent in transporting prisoners are the culprits in murders growing out of these assignments.

Investigating Suspicious Circumstances

It is hard to find reasons why a greater percentage of Oklahoma lawmen were murdered than those nationally while investigating suspicious persons or circumstances. While officers are very inquisitive by nature and training, there is no reason to believe that the state's lawmen are any more so than officers across the United States.

One of the six Oklahoma circumstances is representative of what could happen anywhere, day or night, when officers check out their suspicions. Early one morning, an officer observed a car parked at a service station after hours. He knew that the car had not been there an hour earlier, so he investigated. As he warily approached the car, an occupant blasted the officer with a shotgun. His assailant was convicted and sentenced to life in prison.

Another Oklahoma officer died as he spoke with some men in the parking lot of a tavern. He was doing followup work on a theft reported a day earlier. Suddenly, the father of one of the men stepped up to the officer and, without warning, started shooting. The officer was hit and died instantly, having had no chance to defend himself. His murderer was sentenced to life.

Ambushes

Nationally, the ambush attack did not play a significant role in the killings of police prior to 1969. For example, the FBI reports that during the five years, 1965-69, 14 officers were murdered by attacks from ambush. There were not an appreciable number prior to that year. However, from 1970 to 1978, with two exceptions, the toll year-by-year rose at a disconcerting rate. From 1979 through 1984, the number seems to be stabilizing, but still below the peak years' totals. The year-by-year sums are shown below:

Year	Number	Year	Number
1970	19	1978	12
1971	20	1979	7
1972	14	1980	7
1973	0	1981	6
1974	9	1982	9
1975	10	1983	9
1976	13	1984	8
1977	4		

The dramatic national upsurge for 1970-1972 seems linked to the stepped-up sociopolitical environment, in which police found themselves increasingly involved with the onset of campus unrest, antiwar demonstrations, and street violence.

The Oklahoma picture is the reverse of that nationally. In fact, all four ambush murders on unwary Sooner lawmen occurred relatively early over the 35 years: one death each in 1951, 1954, 1958, and 1962. All were in nonurban places.

Three of the four Oklahoma ambush victims were alone. The one victim who was in the presence of another was, for all intents and purposes, alone, as he was in the company of a nontrained part-time city employee, who was also murdered. Two of the incidents occurred at night, and two during daylight, which suggests that darkness is not necessarily a big ingredient of ambush attacks.

Handling Mentally Deranged Persons

Cases where officers must deal with persons suffering from mental aberrations are among the most difficult for police to handle. These transactions are among the most unpredictable the lawmen face and are usually laden with emotion. One Oklahoma case is illustrative. At 10:30 A.M. one Tuesday in July, a distraught man reported to police that his 74-year-old father had barricaded himself in his house, was armed, and wouldn't come out. The son asked police to help persuade the elderly man to seek medical treatment. Three lawmen drove to the home in two vehicles, the officer who knew the elderly man being the officer alone.

The two officers unfamiliar with the man stopped well away from the house to wait for the son. To the dismay of the two lawmen, the officer who knew the elderly man drove right up to the house. Seeing the elderly man preparing to fire, the officers who were back from the house shouted a warning to the solo officer, who hastily retreated to his car. As he was scrambling in, there was a shot and the officer was dead from a .20 gauge shotgun blast in the forehead. The confused elderly man was later killed by police.

Traffic Pursuits and Stops

That there were no murders stemming from traffic stops or pursuits in Oklahoma for over 20 years, from 1950 to mid-1970, is nothing short of miraculous, especially when thousands of traffic stops are made each month across the state. However, seven officers were murdered in the ensuing 14-1/2 years during this type of activity.

Many traffic stops are made in isolated settings by personnel working alone at night. Moreover, almost all are considered routine by officers, unless their senses are piqued to something unusual. So, while an officer may perceive a traffic stop as routine, it may indeed be what the driver sees as his moment of truth because of some earlier criminal activity of which the officer is not aware. The officer is a sitting duck.

This is what happened in 1970, when a highway patrol trooper was viciously gunned down about 11:45 P.M. near Ardmore in an isolated setting. The trooper didn't know that the speeding driver he had stopped had been involved only hours earlier in a murder and a kidnapping. To the trooper, the stop was routine.

TIME AND PLACE OF THE KILLINGS

When and where officers were murdered is important to know. So are factors as day, month, season, and daylight or darkness. Urban and rural characteristics of the cases should be set out, too, as should the frequency pattern. These factors are described next.

Month, Day, and Hour

Just before midnight in June or July has been the most likely time for lawmen in Oklahoma to be murdered. In fact, 18 of 54 lost their lives during these two summer months. Fourteen of the 16 deaths that occurred in urban areas took place from April through September, usually the warmest periods with the liveliest and loveliest evenings.

Neither the Oklahoma nor the national tabulations of month of the incident are useful in predicting when the next police officer may be murdered. However, at least as pertains to Oklahoma, the figures on month of the incident disclose that warmer ones are when officers face greatest danger. This contrasts sharply with the national picture, as data in Table 4 show.

The most dangerous day of the week is remarkably congruent in both the Oklahoma and national data. Table 5 shows that danger lurks at times other than on weekends, although many people believe that weekends hold more potential for crime. This may be so, but not to the point popularly imagined.

The time when incidents occur is shown in Table 6. With a few exceptions, the Oklahoma data generally correspond with national figures. Most notable, though not a surprise, is that about five of every ten police murders happened between 6 P.M. and 2 A.M., with the most lethal two-hour span being from 10 P.M. to midnight.

Daylight vs. Darkness

Darkness, a phantom time, is another factor which adds to the danger of being attacked. Darkness is seen as a cover by the suspect

Table 4

OKLAHOMA AND NATIONAL INCIDENTS
BY MONTH OF THE YEAR

Month of the Year	1950-1984 Oklahoma Data:		1968-1984* National Data:	
	Number	Percent	Number	Percent
January	3	5.8	168	9.9
February	2	3.8	138	8.1
March	–	–	111	6.5
April	5	9.6	147	8.6
May	7	13.5	150	8.8
June	9	17.3	126	7.4
July	9	17.3	138	8.1
August	1	2.0	145	8.5
September	5	9.6	132	7.8
October	4	7.7	135	7.9
November	2	3.8	139	8.2
December	5	9.6	173	10.2
TOTALS:	52	100.0	1,702	100.0

*The FBI national data for deaths by month are not shown prior to 1968.

Table 5

OKLAHOMA AND NATIONAL INCIDENTS
BY DAY OF THE WEEK

Day of the Week	1950-1984 Oklahoma Data:		1960-1984 National Data:	
	Number	Percent	Number	Percent
Sunday	7	13.5	275	12.9
Monday	8	15.4	292	13.6
Tuesday	5	9.6	273	12.8
Wednesday	6	11.5	291	13.6
Thursday	8	15.4	331	15.5
Friday	9	17.3	343	16.0
Saturday	9	17.3	333	15.6
TOTALS:	52	100.0	2,138	100.0

Table 6

OKLAHOMA AND NATIONAL INCIDENTS
BY HOUR OF THE DAY

Hour of the Day	1950-1984 Oklahoma Data:		1960-1984 National Data:	
	Number	Percent	Number	Percent
12 P.M.- 2A.M.	7	13.5	285	13.4
2A.M.- 4A.M.	3	5.7	224	10.6
4A.M.- 6A.M.	2	3.8	107	5.0
6A.M.- 8A.M.	-	-	58	2.7
8A.M.-10A.M.	3	5.7	100	4.7
10A.M.-NOON	7	13.5	142	6.7
NOON- 2P.M.	-	-	147	6.9
2P.M.- 4P.M.	2	3.8	150	7.1
4P.M.- 6P.M.	3	5.7	168	7.9
6P.M.- 8P.M.	6	11.6	186	8.8
8P.M.-10P.M.	8	15.4	244	11.5
10P.M.-12P.M.	11	21.3	313	14.7
TOTALS:	52	100.0	2,124	100.0

prone to violence. It may also encourage attacks on police because suspects believe that darkness will aid their escape and reduce the chance that their deed will be discovered. The evening hours are the drinking hours, too, and the time when aimless people look for excitement and confrontation. These are the ego hours.

The Oklahoma data give a revealing picture of how daytime-nighttime conditions affect police murders. About two of every three of the 52 incidents occurred under darkness. Two of the 52 encounters were at dusk, in the shadows of the day.

Nighttime was the most dangerous time for officers attempting other arrests, responding to disturbance calls, and investigating suspicious persons or circumstances. The burglaries and robberies-in-progress murders were nighttime incidents, too, as were most traffic stop slayings. By contrast, five of the six transportation murders occurred in daylight.

The Geography of the Killings

Pinpointing just where the killings occurred within the state is important to isolating the urban-rural distinctions in the incidents. This may help explain some of the social variables of police officer murders and contribute to devising effective countermeasures. As a state, Oklahoma is almost 63 percent urban in its population makeup. There are four urbanized regions classified as Metropolitan Statistical Areas (MSAs) by the United States Bureau of the Census. These include 1,890,816 of the state's 3,025,487 resident population, according to the 1980 census. The local MSAs are those regions around and including Oklahoma City (946,958 people); Tulsa (719,732 people); Lawton (124,163 people); and Enid (69,214 people). The 30,749 residents of Sequoyah County in far eastern Oklahoma are classified as part of the Fort Smith, Arkansas MSA.

While the state's population is definitely urban, the geography of Oklahoma's 52 murder incidents is decidedly nonurban. For example, 36 of the 52, or over two of every three incidents, occurred outside the state's MSAs.

The urban-rural distinction reveals a highly significant finding: There is as much danger in rural places as in the cities! Hence, no officer should feel secure from attack merely because he believes he is among friends in the country or small city. Guns abound in rural as well as in urban Oklahoma and, clearly, this hardware is used for more than sport and varmint control!

The 16 urban incidents included three Tulsa officers, five with the Oklahoma City force, and one each from Norman, Catoosa, Spencer, and Oklahoma City's Will Rogers World Airport. In addition, two Oklahoma Highway Patrol troopers were murdered while serving in the Oklahoma City MSA, and two were serving in the Tulsa MSA. No sheriff's personnel were victims in urban areas. On the other hand, the 38 officers murdered in nonurban incidents included 16 from small city forces, 14 from sheriff's departments, and eight highway patrol personnel.

The Murder Weapon

As every officer knows, police all too often must resolve incidents where firearms are involved. It is touchy work, highly volatile, and calls for extraordinary officer presence, judgement, and quick thinking. Table 7 shows that there is an incredible amount of firepower being unleashed on police officers. What's more, if a bullet finds its mark, it is very likely to be fatal. J. Edgar Hoover underscored this fact in the September, 1967 issue of the **FBI Law Enforcement Bulletin:** "The readily available, lethal firearm, seven times more deadly than other murder weapons, is a major factor [in officer killings]."

Table 7

THE NUMBER AND PERCENTAGES OF OFFICERS MURDERED IN OKLAHOMA AND NATIONALLY BY TYPE OF WEAPON

Type of Weapons	Oklahoma: 1950-1984		Nationally: 1960-1984	
	Number	Percent	Number	Percent
Handguns	35	64.8	1,506	70.5
Shotguns	14	25.9	242	11.3
Rifles	3	5.6	266	12.4
Knife, other cutting instrument	–	–	35	1.6
Bomb	–	–	8	.4
Personal Weapons: Hands, Fists, Feet	–	–	16	.8
Other: Clubs, Autos, Etc.	2	3.7	65	3.0
TOTALS:	54	100.0	2,138	100.0

The handgun, by far the most destructive, commonly available lethal weapon police face, was used in 35 of the fatal assaults on Oklahoma lawmen. Long guns—14 shotguns and three rifles—were used in 17 of the murders. An automobile was used to snuff out the lives of two lawmen. That so much of Oklahoma is in cattle, farms, and wheat, may account for the high incidence of shotguns used to kill police in contrast to rifles. Many, many ruralites own shotguns for killing varmints and game hunting, so a shotgun in a pickup truck gun rack is not an uncommon Sooner State sight!

The handguns are a varied array from the staggering arsenal available to the Oklahoma criminal. The death weapons include:

Weapon*	Times Used
.38 Calibre	11
.25 Calibre automatic	7
.32 Calibre automatic	5
.22 Calibre automatic	4
.325 Magnum	1
.357 Magnum	3
.44 Magnum	1
.380 Browning automatic	1
.45 Calibre	1
7.65 Beretta pistol	1
.38 or .357	1

*One officer was shot with two different handguns

Nationally, as in Oklahoma, the handgun is by far the most dangerous weapon police must face while on patrol. Such weapons, highly concealable, are much more likely to be sprung on officers than either shotguns or rifles; weapons not so readily kept from view, but still extraordinarily fatal when used.

Unfortunately, the very weapon a lawman carries for his own protection sometimes turns out to be his worst liability. For example, nationally, over the 18 years, 1967-84, handguns were used in 1,252 murders of lawmen. Of these victims, 225 (or 18.6 percent) lost control of their own personal arms and were murdered with them. In essence, the victim officer had armed an unarmed suspect. During 35 years in Oklahoma, six officers were murdered with their own guns, while two others were killed by guns taken from their partners. These data cry out that an officer wage a titanic struggle before allowing himself to be disarmed!

Distance Between the Officer and Suspect

The shooting erupted suddenly and came at close range in most of the Oklahoma incidents. Quick as a wink, the victim was confronted by a firearm. There was at least one shot, and he was hit. Only a few officers had time to draw their weapons and fire. Death came with practically no warning. Some probably never suspected what was taking place until the first bullet ripped through their body. These characteristics underscore the urgent need for better, more timely safeguards for officers, since, in most cases, police are victimized when they least expect to be.

Table 8 shows that cop killing comes at close quarters. Over 50 percent of victim officers are within a virtual arm's reach of death when hit by bullets. Almost three of every four gunshot hits come from within ten feet! This confirms that the action is often sudden, without warning, and deadly. There is little room for officer error, and there is not much chance for reaction after the first shot. These data, and those in Table 7, confirm that it is handguns, not rifles, shotguns, knives, etc., that take officers out!

The Injuries and Death

In all, the Oklahoma victims took an average of almost two hits each; total shots finding their marks being 91. Even this figure may be a few hits low, owing to one case where the postmortem account was vague, reporting "several hits." Officers were struck by 26 shots in the head/

Table 8

LAW ENFORCEMENT OFFICERS MURDERED IN OKLAHOMA AND NATIONALLY, SHOWING THE DISTANCE BETWEEN THE VICTIM OFFICER AND THE MURDERER

Distance in Feet	Oklahoma: 1950-1984		Nationally: 1972-1984	
	Number	Percent	Number	Percent
0- 5	26	50.0	662	52.4
6-10	10	19.2	261	20.6
11-20	11	21.2	183	14.5
21-50	2	3.8	83	6.6
Over 50	3	5.8	75	5.9
TOTALS:	52	100.0	1,264	100.0

neck region; 54 times in the torso/body; and the victims' arms and legs suffered four wounds. None of the officers were hit in their hands or feet. There were seven shots which hit the victims, but just where was not specified in postmortem accounts.

Close range, the element of surprise, and a hit in at least one vital area were reasons for instantaneous death. Forty-one of the victim Oklahoma officers died either instantaneously or within one hour of the shooting. Nine others died within six hours. One lived 36 hours, while another officer survived six days before succumbing to his wounds.

An officer, gravely wounded but able to shoot his assailant, is a frequent television phenomenon. But does it often occur in the real world? Sometimes, but only one officer in Oklahoma was able to kill his assailant. A few other victims were able to return fire, inflicting nonfatal wounds, while some fired but found no mark. Most victims never got off a shot.

ALONE OR ASSISTED — A RAGING CONTROVERSY

Twenty-seven of the 54 Oklahoma officers were working alone and were unassisted at the time they were murdered. Of the 27 victims who were in the company of other officers when killed, eight were working in one-officer cars; 15 were part of a two-officer patrol team; and three of the victims were detectives when they were fatally wounded.

The last of these 27 victims was a lieutenant who was in a unit with another officer when he was shot.

There were 31 victims murdered under cover of darkness. Of these, 15 were unassisted. There were 21 deaths during daylight hours. In eleven of these, the victims were unassisted. There were two deaths at dusk. In these, one officer was unassisted, and one was being assisted when killed.

Of the 16 victims working in urban places when murdered, three were alone in one-officer units working at night, and five were alone when murdered during the day. Five officers working with partners were slain at night. Three other lawmen in one-officer units were murdered, but these victims were being assisted when killed; two were murdered during daylight, the other was slain at dusk.

Of the 38 officers murdered in nonurban settings, six were unassisted and murdered during daylight, while 12 were alone and murdered during darkness. There was one rural officer who was patrolling alone and was slain at dusk. Twelve rural officers were assisted when murdered at night; seven were daylight victims who fell when in the company of other lawmen.

Dry as these numbers are, they tell the story of lives lost in the line of duty, officers upholding the laws they pledged to enforce. So it is timely to question the assignment of officers, one to a patrol car, to see if that practice contributes to the murder of police officers.

What is striking about the deaths is not the oneness of 27 victims, or that 27 others were in the presence of from one to four other officers, but that many of the murders were preventable. It appears that a lack of training, a moment of carelessness, overreliance on other officers, a guess which proved wrong about how acquaintances were going to behave, and an underestimation of apparent circumstances contributed to several deaths. Failure to comply with some standard communications or field tactical procedure was central to the deaths of some officers, too. These lapses characterized not just some men working singly, but were apparent in cases where several officers were present. The issue, then, is not purely one-vs-two officer patrols. It is far broader.

Owing to the nominal data base involved in the research, absolute conclusions cannot be drawn about one-vs-two officer assignments. But the fact that a few more assisted officers were murdered during the night than were unassisted officers suggests that two personnel in the car are not necessarily safer than an officer alone. At the same time, it cannot be persuasively argued that it is more dangerous to serve in a two-officer patrol team than in a solo unit either, though these teams get into their share of scrapes. There are, of course, disadvantages to patrolling alone. But with today's instantaneous communications, assistance is no more than a radio call away. So the alone-vs-assisted controversy swirls, and this research fails to provide a clear-cut answer to the relative safety of various patrol-staffing patterns.

The only fact about one- and two-officer motor patrols proved by the Oklahoma study is the near certainty that the issue will surface with intensity and emotion when an officer alone is murdered. The issue can become politicized, too. For example, soon after a highway patrol trooper was murdered north of Altus, Oklahoma's then governor announced that the probe of the shooting would include studying the patrol's policy of having troopers cruise alone. In the wake of another trooper's murder, an Ardmore legislator coauthored a bill (which failed to pass), making two-officer patrolling mandatory at night in cities over 10,000 population. The death of yet another trooper prompted the chief of the Oklahoma Highway Patrol at that time to state that the incident emphasized the need for two troopers in the cars at all times. At once, the then governor announced a plan to put troopers out in pairs, but nothing of any substance happened in the wake of the apparent political hoopla. After a few weeks, troopers patrolled alone, by their choice.

These three incidents characterize this continuing controversy. On one side is the theory that there is safety in numbers. Advocates of one-officer patrols, on the other hand, assert that proper training, constant vigilance, and ever-present radio communications provide the unassisted officer a safety net with all the advantages of two-officer patrol, while at the same time intensifying area coverage and maximizing officer visibility.

The issue remains open, highly contentious, and certain to surface again, again, and again. Especially in the wake of a murder where the officer was serving alone.

CHAPTER II

THE ACTORS: COPS AND KILLERS

EACH FORCE wonders if one of its personnel will be the next to suffer a fatal injury. Of course, they hope not. However, inevitably, murders will occur and other Oklahoma lawmen will suffer, as 54 did between 1950 and 1985.

After finding out what happened, who's involved? What are the characteristics of the victims and suspects? Are there any common denominators? Were the actors acquainted before the event? Is there a racial angle? Preincident antagonism?

POLICE OFFICER VICTIMS

He is an Oklahoma native, white, in uniform, serving as a trooper, deputy or police officer, and about 41 years of age. If he is not an Oklahoma Highway Patrol trooper, he works for a small non-urban force, is married, has two youngsters, and has been a police officer for almost seven years. He has served in the armed forces, is a high school graduate and has had some college hours, but no degree. He was on auto patrol, but other officers were at hand, working in the early evening on Friday or Saturday. He was cut down by sudden gunfire and died within one hour of the incident. This profile sets out the "typical" victim, although, understandably, no two victims or incidents are the same.

Sex and Race

All 54 Oklahoma victim officers were male. Of the 54, 49 were white, one was an American Indian, and four were black. The four black officers were murdered by black assailants, while the Indian officer, a sheriff, was murdered by an American Indian. Of the 49 white officers, 37 were murdered by whites, ten by blacks and two by Indians.

Women, who only since about 1975 have attained equal footing with males in police departments across the United States, comprise but a modest portion of the law enforcement work force. For example, in 1984, the FBI reported that only six percent of the nation's 467,117 sworn police officers were female. However, police departments are actively inducting, training, and assigning greater numbers of female police officers to street patrol duty, so their number is increasing. Oklahoma has never had a female police officer murdered on duty and very few have been victims of nonfatal assaults. In fact, not many forces nationwide have had a female killed. But some are being assaulted and a few murdered, too. The **job** and its very nature, **not gender,** is the issue when women officers are slain.

The nation's first female officer murder victim was a 24-year-old black officer with one year of service with the District of Columbia police. Ms. Gail A. Cobb was on foot patrol in September, 1974, when a citizen told her that two armed and wanted men were hiding in an underbuilding parking lot after having exchanged gunfire with other officers. The officer, who came from a family where police jobs were a tradition, entered the garage and was fatally wounded with a .38 calibre handgun. Two suspects were subsequently arrested.

Houston's first female officer was killed under especially distressing circumstances. She was accidentally shot and killed while in plainclothes on an undercover drug investigation. Something went sour when the victim and a male counterpart were making a drug buy and gunshots erupted. She was shot by a uniformed Houston officer who observed the transaction and felt he was placed in a life-threatening situation. Seven months earlier, a Montgomery, Alabama, female officer, also in a plainclothes, undercover assignment, was shot to death while she and her partner attempted an arrest.

The first female officer in New York City's history to be murdered on duty was a 25-year-old Transit Authority officer with three years of service. She was slain on September 21, 1984, shot twice in the head with her own revolver. Her body was found in a weed-choked vacant lot in the Bushwick section of Brooklyn three hours after she and her male partner had split up to chase a suspected gold-chain snatcher. A 19-year-old male suspect was indicted six days later.

The first female federal officer murdered while on duty was a U.S. Secret Service agent who, with a partner, was conducting a surveillance during a Los Angeles investigation. On the evening of June 4, 1980, the two agents, in plainclothes, were victims of an apparent robbery attempt. Forced from the surveillance vehicle, the victim agent was disarmed and murdered with the .12 gauge shotgun she was carrying. The first FBI female agent was killed in Phoenix, Arizona, on October 5, 1985, while helping other agents arrest an armed robbery suspect. She was the first female to die in the line of duty since women became agents in 1972.

Forces other than big ones, like the District of Columbia, Houston, Montgomery, and New York City, have suffered female officer fatalities. Among these are female sworn members serving Baton Rouge, Louisiana; Aurora, Colorado; Overland Park, Kansas; Huntsville, Texas; and Plainfield, New Jersey. So, too, have the police of San Diego, California; Denver, Colorado; and the Florida Game and Freshwater Fish Commission.

More and more females are joining police forces as officers. Some are being promoted. In fact, Portland, Oregon, was the first major American city to name a female as police chief in March, 1985, when Penny Ledyard Orazetti Harrington was selected from among several candidates.

Birthplace

Data assembled principally from death certificates revealed the birthplace of each of the 54 officer victims. Thirty-six were born in Oklahoma and apparently chose to work near the place of their birth, rejecting the pattern of out-migration which characterized many Oklahomans, beginning in the 1920s, and which John Steinbeck vividly described in his classic novel, **The Grapes of Wrath.** That many of these 36 native-born Oklahomans were United States military veterans and served on posts across the nation, as well as worldwide, but after service chose to return to settings where they felt comfortable, safe, and at ease, underscores how really local these slain officers were.

The data also reveal that not uncommonly the victims were murdered at a site relatively near where they were born many years earlier. In fact, 29 of the 54 officers were murdered within 100 miles of their birthplace and of these, 13 were victimized within 25 miles! Only six of the 54 were murdered at a locale farther than 500 miles from their place of birth.

Rank

Although 43 Oklahoma police officers, troopers, city marshals, and deputy sheriffs were killed, persons in higher ranks were by no means safe. Among executives, five chiefs of police or sheriffs were killed, as was one assistant chief, one undersheriff, and one lieutenant. Three detective or uniformed sergeants were felled by gunfire, too. So police are murdered, irrespective of rank or role.

Age

Not just young, inexperienced officers were killed in Oklahoma. The average age of the 54 at time of their death was 41 years, 3 months. Checking extremes, one officer was murdered just four days before his 23rd birthday, while two others were but 24 years old. On the other hand, one sheriff's deputy was 69 when murdered in 1972 while intervening in a stickup in progress. The victims, by age range, are set out below:

Age Range	Number of Officers	Percentage
21-25	5	9.3
26-30	11	20.4
31-35	4	7.4
36-40	8	14.8
41-45	4	7.4
46-50	7	13.0
51-55	8	14.8
56-60	4	7.4
61-65	1	1.8
66-	2	3.7
TOTAL		100.0

The number of officers murdered by five-year blocks over the past 35 years and their average age is shown below:

Years	Number of Officers Murdered	Average Age
1950-54	13	46.1
1955-59	4	46.0
1960-64	7	38.4
1965-69	4	41.0
1970-74	13	38.5
1975-79	9	44.8
1980-84	4	27.0
35 years	54	41.3

The data above show two five-year blocks when 13 officers were murdered, and a third (1975-79) which approached the years of greatest lethality. However, there is no consistent pattern. Neither is there a consistent pattern to the age of the victims, although the officers murdered from 1980-84 averaged 19 years less in age than the victims of the 1950s.

The 16 officers serving in urban settings when murdered averaged 35.4 years of age. Their 38 nonurban counterparts averaged 43.0 years of age. The fact that the nonurban officers are much older than the urban ones may be a reflection of less stringent police service entry requirements and less attractive retirement programs in the nonurban forces.

The average age of the 12 murdered highway patrol troopers was 36.9, while sheriff's personnel averaged 46.3 years of age when killed. Municipal police victims were 40.6 years of age.

Marital Status

The 54 Oklahoma victim police officers were, save two divorced and two others who had never been wedded, a married lot. The death of these 54 lawmen left 116 children fatherless. Several of the surviving children were, however, adults with their own families. One of the officers had been married but a few months, while a veteran highway patrol trooper had been married 43 years. A county sheriff left seven children fatherless when he was murdered.

It is a popular notion, probably based on mortality figures of American servicemen killed in World War II, the Korean War, and the Vietnamese conflict, that single men will take greater risks with their lives than will married men. Or as sometimes framed, a married man will be more cautious than a single man who has no home-front ties to inhibit his actions. By no means are these notions upheld by the Oklahoma experience.

Whether being married had anything to do with an officer's degree of caution or reluctance to take chances as circumstances unfold is speculative. The data in this study neither confirm nor reject this premise, but they do underscore that an officer of any age may be called upon to face a dangerous situation at any time or place. This is especially so in rural locales where each officer wears many hats.

Prior Law Enforcement Experience

The number of years that lawmen had served was determined for 44 of the 54 Oklahoma officers. Their average length of service was 6.8

years, although more than 23 of the personnel had less than five years with their parent force.

Several seasoned personnel fell prey to cop killers. Two highway patrol troopers had, respectively, 32 and 25 years service when they were murdered by two vicious escapees from McAlester Penitentiary over the Memorial Day weekend of 1978. A police chief was just finishing his 22nd year in law enforcement when he lost his life responding to a disturbance call. Another officer was on the job only two weeks prior to being gunned down, but he was not inexperienced, having held police posts in other cities for several years. Similarly, another chief had been with his force about a year when murdered, but he had had 17 years prior experience after seven years as a United States Marine. He was hardly inexperienced! One officer was inexperienced: he had only six months service when he died from a shotgun wound suffered during an arrest attempt.

These data show that mere years in law enforcement do not automatically weave a cloak of protection around an officer. But what may be concluded from these figures is that an officer reaches peak exposure to criminal activity during his fifth or sixth year of service. This picture corresponds with FBI accounts of officer victimization as well as with information derived from the Oklahoma University Police Assaults Study of over 1,100 incidents in 1973.[1]

Military Service

Twenty-seven of the 54 victims had prior military experience, 19 had had none, and there were eight officers about whom no military information could be obtained. Military service dates from World War I duty to several men who were combat veterans of World War II, Korea, and the Vietnamese war. Some were decorated veterans.

Educational Achievement

Information as to education was obtained for only 34 of the 54 officers. Two had earned bachelor's degrees and 13 had been educated beyond high school but had not been awarded a four-year degree. Sixteen

---

[1]This project was supported by the Law Enforcement Assistance Administration under Grant Numbers 73-TA-06-004 and 73-DF-06-0053. A three-volume **Final Report** and an **Operations Research Manual** were published on June 28, 1974, by the Bureau of Government Research at the University of Oklahoma.

were high school graduates with no subsequent education, while three did not complete high school. Officers who were murdered from 1970 onward were significantly more highly educated than persons victimized earlier.

SUSPECTS

Many assumptions are made about cop killers. They are generally characterized as hardened, insensitive, cold-blooded killers, lacking any sense of compassion or guilt. Moreover, they are often said to be drug-crazed and to have long criminal records. By no means are these assumptions universally accurate.

When profiled, the 69 suspects resemble their 54 victims in a few respects. For example, they are white males, about 31.5 years of age, born in Oklahoma, and living in nonurban areas of the state. But suspects differ from their victims in many ways. They are not as well educated. Not all had jobs. Those who did, held blue-collar-type jobs. Many, many of the suspects had been drinking or were under the influence of alcohol or other drugs at the time of the incident. Finally, many — but by no means all — of the suspects had been arrested at least once prior to the fatal confrontation, and some had been in jail or prison prior to the incident. Five were jail or prison escapees, very badly wanted by police.

These are not surprising characteristics describing a group of persons who cop fight. The exceptional thing is that the average age of a cop killer is almost eight years older than the average age of persons arrested for murder nationally.

There is neither a clear-cut, easily identifiable type of suspect, nor is a cop killer an atavistic, animallike breed of man or woman. The person is a truck driver, a cab driver, a waitress, a laborer, a barber, or unemployed, among other things. The suspect may have had a year and a half of college or no formal education at all. He may be white, black, or Indian, and he may not be a he, but rather female! All of this signals that an officer should never be lulled into a sense of security and should never assume that the person with whom the lawman is currently dealing will not suddenly become violent.

Sex and Race

Almost all — 66 of 69 — suspects were male. Of the males, 45 were white, 17 were black, and four were Indian. Of the three females, one was black, one was white, and one was an Indian.

Contrary to popular stereotype, most of the murder suspects were not black. On the national level, between 1964-84, there were slightly more whites than blacks identified as suspects. Until 1980, the national data gave heed to ethnicity only in terms of black or white, grouping Indians and Hispanics with whites. Table 9 sets out the ethnicity of police officer murder suspects.

Table 9
THE ETHNICITY OF POLICE OFFICER
MURDER SUSPECTS

Race	Oklahoma 1950-1984		Nationwide 1964-1984	
	Number	Percent	Number	Percent
White	46	66.7	1,388	51.6
Black	18	26.1	1,256	46.7
Indian	5	7.2	NG	–
Other			46	1.7
TOTALS:	69	100.0	2,690	100.0

Of the 13,656 persons arrested nationally during 1984 for all types of murders, 53.7 percent were white; 44.9 percent were black; 0.7 percent were American Indian; and 0.7 percent were Asian. None of the national data about persons who murder police or who commit other classes of murder support the notion that blacks are cop killers notably more so than others.

Of the 23 suspects in the 16 urban murders, 14 were white, eight were black, and there was one Indian female. Of the 46 suspects in the 38 nonurban murders, 31 were white males. There were nine black males and four male Indian suspects, in addition to two white female suspects involved in nonurban incidents.

Birthplace

Thirty-three, or almost one of every two of the killers, were born in Oklahoma, while 36 were born in one of 14 other states. None were born outside the United States. Seventeen suspects were from Texas; three each from Arkansas and Missouri; two each from Kansas and

Indiana; and one each from Arizona, Colorado, Mississippi, New York, North Dakota, North Carolina, Ohio, Tennessee, and Virginia.

Two of the out-of-state suspects were AWOL servicemen, and one was an escaped convict from North Carolina. That only two of 36 suspects were from states west of Oklahoma (Colorado and Arizona), suggests that there are few folks who come to Oklahoma once they have savored the virtues of the nation's western slope!

Age

The national trend shows the overwhelming involvement of youth 18 years of age and under in crime. This failed to surface in the composite picture of Oklahoma police officer murder suspects. In fact, the suspects were, generally speaking, between the ages of 20 and 29. The youngest suspect was 16. Another was 17. The oldest were two white males, both 74. The average age of the 69 Oklahoma suspects was 31.1 years. The

Table 10

THE NUMBER OF SUSPECTS BY AGE RANGES
IN THE MURDER OF OKLAHOMA POLICE
1950-1984

Age Range	Number of Suspects	Percentage of Suspects in Range	Percentage of Oklahoma's 1980 Population in Range
0-14	–	–	22.9
15-19	6	8.7	9.2
20-24	23	33.3	9.4
25-29	15	21.7	8.3
30-34	6	8.7	7.5
35-39	4	5.8	6.0
40-44	5	7.2	5.2
45-49	2	2.9	4.8
50-54	2	2.9	5.0
55-59	2	2.9	5.0
60-64	1	1.5	4.3
65-69	1	1.5	4.0
70-74	2	2.9	3.4
75+	0	–	5.0
TOTALS:	69	100.0	100.0

two 74-year-olds were both involved in nonurban incidents and both were killed at the scene. One of the suspects was reportedly suffering mental difficulties prior to the incident, while the other suddenly went berserk. The age ranges of the Oklahoma suspects is shown in Table 10.

Educational Achievement

Educational achievement information for only 39 of the suspects was found. Eight suspects were high school graduates. However, the average level of schooling for all suspects was about nine and one-half years, or freshman in high school level. A black suspect was the most highly educated, having completed one and one-half years of college. Two urban and two rural suspects had had one year of college. The least educated was the 69-year old black slayer of a black Ardmore police officer who, according to prison records, had had no formal education whatsoever. Information about 13 of the 17 suspects involved in urban murders revealed that these men were slightly better educated than their rural counterparts. Their average level of education was that of a junior in high school.

Occupation and Employment

Of the 69 suspects, 29 were employed at the time of the incident, 16 were unemployed, and the employment status of 12 suspects was unknown. Of the other 12 offenders, two were AWOL servicemen, two were retired people, five were jail/prison escapees, two were students, and one was a disabled person. That several suspects were unemployed at the time of the murder matches a larger picture wherein criminal behaviorists traditionally cite the lack of work as contributing to antisocial behavior.

The most common occupation of the suspects was that of laborer, but the following roles had been the livelihood of one or more of the slayers:

Truck/equipment driver	Warehouseman	Painter
Laborer	Boilermaker	Prize fighter
Farmer	Carpenter	Salesman
Welder	Oilfield machinist	School bus driver
Mechanic	Brick layer	Taxi cab driver
Barber	Crop duster pilot	Tree surgeon
Armed forces	Domestic worker	Trucking executive
Construction worker	Office clerk	Upholsterer
Electrician		Waitress

Alcohol and Other Drug Use

Alcohol and the use of other drugs plays an important role in the murder of officers. Although drug use itself cannot be labeled "the cause" of police slayings, it is a contributing factor to the carnage. Through it, inhibitions are lessened. The short person, the young adult, the unemployed individual, or the minority group member who perceives himself as enslaved, might feel threatened. When drugs reduce inhibitions, aggressive behavior may be directed towards others. In the Oklahoma study, the person seen to be blocking opportunities was the police officer. His murder ensued.

It is certain that in 15 of the 52 incidents suspects either had been drinking heavily or were under the influence of alcohol or other drugs. In about 20 other incidents it appears that suspects had consumed alcohol immediately before the incident, but the level of intake was undetermined. In only 17 of the incidents was it certain that alcohol or other drugs were not a factor in the slaying. These figures confirm that the relationship between drugs and assaults on police officers parallels the long-recognized relationship between drug abuse and violence.

PAST CRIMINAL HISTORY

What kind of a rap sheet did the persons who murdered Oklahoma lawmen have? Are police murderers hardened criminals with extensive arrest records or are they small-time hoods, characters who are local nuisances, hardly deserving the title of criminal? Or are people who killed Oklahoma police like anyone else, except once they drank too much they came to a confrontation with authorities and violence ensued?

In order to find out who killed cops in Oklahoma, data were extracted from the official criminal history records for 63 of the 69 suspects. Six suspects were never fingerprinted by the authorities, who apparently felt that it was unnecessary and would serve no useful purpose since five of the six either were killed by police at the time of the incident or committed suicide. The sixth, critically wounded during the incident, lived out his days in a state mental hospital.

When all the tallying is done and each of the 63 suspects is put under a criminal history microscope, it is apparent that as a group they are people who had a bad day, got fogged up on drugs, and ended up murdering police. Only six of the 63 were what police would class as "heavies." Five others were potentially violent and warranted great caution. These included one who was a fugitive felon from North Carolina, just passing through, while four others were very hot escapees from penal facilities in the Sooner State who, when faced by police, didn't want to surrender. The other 52 were, at worst, unskilled thieves or novice stickup men who bungled not-too-complicated heists. Some suspects apparently suffered from mental aberrations and befuddled their minds with alcohol or other drugs before the confrontation which took a police life. In short, data disclose that the small-time criminal arrested once or twice for non-violent crimes was the person most likely to murder an Oklahoma police officer.

Several interesting findings surfaced. These are reported below, based on the 63 persons for whom the nature and extent of official prior criminal involvement and convictions was able to be ascertained.

What Suspects Were Arrested For

As Table 11 shows, with some notable individual exceptions, most of the 63 suspects did not have much in the way of prior criminal records. In fact, the table shows that the suspects averaged just over two felony arrests each. Moreover, on only 148 occasions were the 63 suspects taken into police custody for misdemeanor, traffic, or other reasons.

Surprisingly, 17 of the 63 suspects had never been arrested at all prior to the lawmen's murder! On the other extreme, one man, 24 years of age, had been arrested 37 times, 16 being for felony offenses, before he ended his career by murdering an Oklahoma City officer. The next heaviest suspect murdered a deputy sheriff and a citizen in Oklahoma's panhandle early one morning as the two investigated suspicious circumstances. This murderer had been arrested 12 times previously, 11 of these being for felonies. He and his co-killer were escapees from the Wagoner County jail in eastern Oklahoma.

Burglary—a crime of stealth—was the offense for which most of the police killers had been arrested before they took a lawman's life. Twenty-three suspects were arrested 41 times for the offense. Twelve urban suspects were arrested 17 times for it. One particular suspect was arrested four different times for burglary.

That burglary is the crime for which so many suspects are arrested is neither unique nor surprising. After all, of the eight index crimes set out

Table 11

THE NUMBER OF PRIOR ARRESTS, BY THE TYPE OF INCIDENT ATTRIBUTABLE TO 63 SUSPECTS IN THE 1950-1984 SLAYING OF 54 OKLAHOMA LAWMEN*

Type of Incident	Number of Incidents for Which Suspects Were Arrested	Actual Number of Suspects Arrested for the Type of Incident	Percent of the 63 Suspects Who Have Been Arrested By Type of Incident
Murder/Manslaughter	3	3	4.8
Rape/Sodomy	3	3	4.8
Robbery	21	12	19.0
Aggravated Assault	10	10	15.9
Weapons Offenses	7	6	9.5
Burglary	41	23	36.5
Forgery/Checks	11	8	12.7
Grand Theft	13	11	17.5
Auto Theft	25	12	19.0
Narcotics	10	6	9.5
Train Wrecking	1	1	1.6
Other Felonies	8	7	11.1
Total Felonies:	153	Average Felonies per Suspect:	2.4
Simple Assault	3	2	3.2
Petty Theft	9	7	11.1
Plain Drunk	15	10	15.9
DUI/DWI	8	5	7.9
Other Liquor	4	3	4.8
Vagrancy/Loitering	27	8	12.7
Disorderly Conduct	5	2	3.2
Other Traffic	12	7	11.1
Other Misdemeanor	9	9	14.3
Resisting Arrest and Assault of an Officer	8	7	12.7
Evading Arrest	1	1	1.6
Escape From Custody	18	10	15.9
Contempt of Court	1	1	1.6
Investigation	16	11	17.5
Other/Unknown	12	8	12.7
Total Misdemeanors and Other Incidents:	148	Average Misdemeanors per Suspect:	2.3
ARRESTS FOR SOME INCIDENT:	301	Average Arrests for Some Incident Per Suspect:	4.8

*Source: These data were extracted from federal and state criminal history records for each of the 63 suspects. Data shown in tables have been derived from the same sources.

by the FBI in its crime reporting program (murder, forcible rape, robbery, aggravated assault, burglary, larceny-theft, auto theft, and arson), burglary constitutes about 25 percent of the total crimes reported each year to the police. But it is interesting that burglary, a crime most consider to be passive and nonviolent in nature, is the crime for which the greatest number of 63 suspected cop killers have been arrested over a 35-year span in a midwestern state.

In the misdemeanor category, arrests for vagrancy/loitering were the most common. A female murderer was the principal contributor to that category, as she had been arrested 11 times for vagrancy, owing to her alleged activities as a prostitute in a southwestern Oklahoma town. The second highest category—drunkenness—accounted for 15 arrests, in which ten suspects—one urban and nine nonurbans—were involved.

Only 40 of the 63 suspects had been arrested for a felony. Some of these men and women were arrested more than once on separate occasions for serious offenses. Only 37 of the 63 had been taken into custody for a misdemeanor charge. As with arrests for felonies, several suspects had multiple arrests.

The sum of arrests for violent crimes is modest. The 63 suspects totalled only three arrests for murder, three for rape, and ten for aggravated assault. There were but seven arrests for weapons offenses, and only five prior arrests for resisting arrest, three for assaulting an officer, three for simple assault, and one for train wrecking. While many of the 63 suspects had arrest records, by no means did they, as a group, have the kind of crime background that would cause the ordinary police officer to expect the violence and aggression associated with police assault.

Nationally, from 1964-1984, there were 2,690 persons identified in the killing of police officers, shown in Table 12. Certain characteristics unique to these persons may be contrasted with the 63 Sooner State suspects. Far fewer Oklahoma suspects had preincident weapons law violations and narcotics arrests than the national group. On the other hand, Oklahoma suspects did more cop fighting than the national group.

Criminal history sheets disclose that only four of the 63 suspects, or 6.3 percent, were on probation or parole at the time they murdered an officer. A fifth suspect had recently completed his parole. Nationally, Table 12 shows that 18.5 percent of the persons identified in the murders of police officers were on parole or probation when an officer was killed. This comparison underscores the finding that persons who murdered Oklahoma lawmen were not, as a group, desperate career criminals, notwithstanding the fact that six of the murderers were very, very seasoned, ugly criminals, and five others were escapees.

Table 12

A PROFILE OF PERSONS IDENTIFIED IN THE KILLING OF POLICE OFFICERS IN OKLAHOMA 1950-1984 AND NATIONWIDE 1964-1984

Factor Unique to Persons Identified	Oklahoma		Nationally	
	Persons Identified	% of Total Persons Identified	Persons Identified	% of Total Persons Identified
Total Number of Persons Identified in Killings:	63	100.0	2,690	100.0
Prior Criminal Arrest	46	73.0	1,971	73.3
Prior Arrest for Crime of Violence	25	39.7	1,009	37.5
On Parole or Probation at Time of Killing	4	6.3	498	18.5
Prior Arrest for Murder	3	4.8	120	4.5
Prior Arrest for Drug Law Violation	6	9.5	445	16.5
Prior Arrest for Assaulting an Officer or Resisting Arrest	7	11.1	227	8.4
Prior Arrest for Weapons Law Violation	6	9.5	640	23.8

Urban vs. Nonurban Arrest Patterns

Only seven of the 22 urban suspects had never been arrested, as compared with ten nonurban suspects who had never been taken into custody prior to murdering an Oklahoma police officer. Fourteen of 22 urban suspects and 25 of 41 nonurban suspects had prior arrests for one or more felony offenses. Eleven of 22, and 27 of 41 nonurban suspects had been arrested for one or more misdemeanor offenses.

Urban suspects had far heavier arrest records than their rural counterparts, having an average of 3.9 felony arrests per suspect. The nonurban suspects averaged 2.3 felony arrests per person, not an inconsequential number for countryfolk. The urban suspects topped their nonurban counterparts in misdemeanor and other arrests, too, averaging 2.7 per suspect, in contrast to 2.1 for those from the state's less densely populated areas. Cumulatively, the urban suspects averaged 6.6 arrests, while the nonurban group averaged far fewer—3.9 arrests per suspect.

There were several suspects whose heavy records inflated the averages. For example, one urban suspect had one arrest for rape, two for robbery, one for aggravated assault, two each for weapons offenses, burglary, and plain drunk. The same man had been arrested eight times for auto theft, five for vagrancy/loitering, four for disorderly conduct, once each for resisting arrest and evading arrest, and twice each for escape from custody and assault on an officer. This totalled 37 arrests—16 for felonies and 21 for misdemeanors. His criminal history alone accounts for 12.3 percent of all 301 arrests for all 63 suspects!

About Convictions

By no means does arrest automatically mean a suspect will be convicted. This is dramatically demonstrated in Table 13, which shows a summary of the arrests-convictions picture for the 63 suspects regarding felonies, and in Table 14 as pertains to misdemeanors.

Table 13

**TOTAL PREINCIDENT ARRESTS AND
CONVICTIONS FOR FELONIES**

(1) Total Suspects	(2) Number Never Arrested for A Felony	(3) Number Having a Felony Arrest	(4) Number Having a Felony Conviction
63	24	39	28

Table 14

TOTAL PREINCIDENT ARRESTS AND
CONVICTIONS FOR MISDEMEANORS

(1) Total Suspects	(2) Number Never Arrested for a Misdemeanor	(3) Number Having a Misdemeanor Arrest	(4) Number Having a Misdemeanor Conviction
63	26	37	22

Table 14 enlarges upon column (4) in both Tables 13 and 14. Table 15 shows the frequency of prior convictions for both felony and misdemeanor offenses. Percentages, also shown, are remarkably low, for well over one-half of all suspects have never been convicted of **either** a felony or misdemeanor. In fact, almost two of every three suspects have **never** been convicted after being arrested! The significance of Table 15 is that by no means have Oklahoma suspects been often convicted following their arrests. And, as shown earlier, they are not characterized as a group by being arrested very often, considering that they ended up murdering police officers.

Table 15

THE FREQUENCY OF PRIOR CONVICTIONS
OF 63 SUSPECTS

Convictions

Class of Offense	No Convictions		One		Two		Three		Four or More		Total	
	No.	Pct.	No.	Pct.	No.	Pct.	No.	Pct.	No.	Pct.	No.	Pct.
Felony	35	55.6	11	17.4	10	15.9	3	4.8	4	6.3	63	100.0
Misdemeanor	41	65.1	6	9.5	9	14.3	1	1.6	6	9.5	63	100.0

Table 16 shows the number of persons convicted, and how many times, by offense. If the number of convictions is contrasted with the number of arrests set out earlier in Table 11, a picture emerges which underscores how rare convictions actually are. For instance, there were only 13 convictions for burglary after 41 arrests. Only ten suspects were actually convicted for burglary (meaning some were convicted twice) as opposed to the 26 suspects who were arrested on burglary charges. The highest number of convictions (21) was for the offense of vagrancy/ loitering. Five suspects (eight had originally been arrested) suffered conviction, and one female suspect had ten of the 21 convictions. A perfect conviction rate was recorded for the three prior murder arrests.

Table 16

THE NUMBER OF PRIOR CONVICTIONS BY OFFENSE FOR 63 SUSPECTS

Type of Offense	Number of Convictions	Number Convicted	Percent of 63
Murder/Manslaughter	3	3	4.8
Rape/Sodomy	1	1	1.6
Robbery	6	5	7.9
Aggravated Assault	3	3	4.8
Weapons Offenses	3	3	4.8
Burglary	13	10	15.9
Forgery/Checks	6	5	7.9
Grand Theft	12	11	17.5
Auto Theft	13	8	12.7
Narcotics	3	3	4.8
Train Wrecking	1	1	1.6
Other Felonies	2	2	3.2
Total Felonies:	66		
Simple Assault	2	1	1.6
Petty Theft	3	3	4.8
Plain Drunk	11	7	11.1
DUI/DWI	5	3	4.8
Other Liquor	1	1	1.6
Vagrancy/Loitering	21	5	7.9
Disorderly Conduct	2	1	1.6
Other Traffic	8	3	4.8
Resisting Arrest and Assault of an Officer	5	5	7.9
Escape from Custody	7	4	6.3
Contempt of Court Officer	1	1	1.6
Other/Unknown	2	2	3.2
Total Misdemeanors and Other Incidents:	68		
Convicted of Something:	134		

Twenty-seven of 63 suspects had never been convicted of any offense prior to their fatal encounter with the police. At the other extreme, a 24-year-old man had been convicted of five felonies and eight misdemeanors. The felony counts were four for auto theft and a weapons offense. This man had been sentenced to prison on four occasions, to pay fines on eight convictions, and had had one felony sentence suspended.

None of the three men who had previously been arrested and convicted for murder were among the two who were executed for murdering an Oklahoma lawman. One of the men with an earlier murder conviction had only a single previous arrest — for drunk driving for which he was convicted, fined, and sentenced to the county jail. Another previous murderer earlier had been arrested and convicted of aggravated assault and faced five earlier misdemeanor charges, including two for drunk driving. He had been convicted following every arrest. The third murderer had twice been charged and convicted of check offenses, by no means an aggressive offense. All three previous murderers were from rural Oklahoma and their encounters with police were in the country, too.

Convicted of murder previous to killing the officer, how was it that these three suspects were out of prison? One had been convicted of murder in Tulsa in 1919 and sentenced to 20 years. Then he murdered an Ardmore police officer in 1958, well after expiration of the original sentence. Another suspect was sentenced to ten years in 1947 for manslaughter in Muskogee, but was released from McAlester Penitentiary in 1952. He murdered a Claremore police officer two years later and took his own life at the incident scene rather than submit to arrest. The third person was convicted of first degree manslaughter in 1975 and was doing 50 years in McAlester Penitentiary. He and a violent fellow inmate broke out of McAlester on April 23, 1978, and went on a vicious crime spree. It ended on Memorial Day weekend of 1978 when both escapees were killed in a shoot-out with police, but not until they had gunned down three highway patrol personnel. It was the worst day in highway patrol history.

A review of the prior records of the two men electrocuted for murdering police is revealing. Only one had a record which was beginning to assume noticeable proportion. He had but one arrest for a crime of violence, a resisting arrest charge for which he was convicted. He had three burglary arrests, too, but no convictions. The second murderer who was executed had been arrested on three prior occasions—once each for aggravated assault, plain drunk and drunk driving—but had never been convicted.

Sentencing

After conviction comes sentencing. Sentencing patterns stemming from convictions of 36 persons for offenses of all sorts are set out in Table 17. What the table shows is how many suspects were fined, given suspended sentences, sent to prison, etc. For example, 25 of the 36 suspects were sentenced to prison, 17 were fined, and six were given a suspended sentence. Then, the table depicts the cumulative number of times the 36 suspects were sentenced by type of disposition. For example, 17 suspects were fined a total of 50 times, roughly 3.0 fines for each person, while 25 were sentenced to prison a total of 61 times, or an average of about 2.5 times per suspect, etc.

Table 17

**THE NUMBER OF SUSPECTS SENTENCED AND
THE CUMULATED NUMBER OF SENTENCES
BY TYPE OF DISPOSITION FOR
36 SUSPECTS***

Type of Disposition	Number of Suspects Sentenced	Cumulative Number of Sentences	Average Number of Sentences Per Suspect
Released to Parents	1	1	1.0
Fined	17	50	2.9
Probation	2	2	1.0
Suspended Sentence	6	7	1.2
County Jail	9	9	1.0
Prison	25	61	2.4
Parole	12	12	1.0
TOTAL DISPOSITIONS	72	142	

*Twenty-seven of the 63 suspects had never been convicted. Hence, this table shows sentences for 36 suspects. The number of sentences is substantially in excess of 36 because several persons, over their criminal career, were sentenced to several differing types of punishment.

CHAPTER III

FROM ARREST TO DISPOSITION

ONCE ARRESTED, there are logical steps for the authorities to follow in the justice process. These include arraignment, representation by counsel, bail, and the preliminary hearing. Then there is the trial, and should there be a conviction, sentencing.

When a cop killer is arrested, police want to get the suspect to trial as soon as possible after the prosecutor has assembled the case. However, sometimes cases drag on, snagged on procedural questions and motions. This is delay, and officers generally believe the greater the delay, the less likely the chance of conviction. Moreover, if it takes a long time to convict a suspect, officers worry that the sentence may not fit the severity of the act of killing a cop. Indeed, many police officers feel that if cases take a long time from arrest to disposition that criminals get a sense that "nothing happens" to police killers. Delay, then, may encourage aggression against police. Conversely, where there is a quick capture and conviction, followed by a harsh penalty for killing police, criminals may think twice before cop fighting. This may alter attacks on police and suggest that society supports its lawmen.

Judicial proceedings were no issue to the 12 Oklahoma cop killers who were either slain by police or took their own lives. But 57 others were arrested and faced the criminal justice process, charged with the following offenses:

Murder in the first degree	53
Murder in the second degree	1
First degree manslaughter	2
Second degree manslaughter	1
	57

45

The verdicts came out as follows:

Murder in the first degree	38
Murder in the second degree	2
First degree manslaughter	6
Second degree manslaughter	1
Charges dismissed	6
Acquitted	2
Died or killed before trial	2
	57

GETTING TO TRIAL

There are as many opportunities for delay in an Oklahoma criminal case as there are in any other state. However, almost all Oklahoma police officer murder suspects were processed from arrest through trial with relative speed. In fact, 42 of the 47 suspects who were sentenced after trial were sentenced within one year of the incident! Moreover, speed did not compromise the suspects' right to due process because only one of the 47 convictions was later overturned by the Oklahoma Court of Criminal Appeals.

The shortest time from the incident to sentencing was 34 days, a case in which an AWOL airman pleaded guilty to murdering a sheriff's deputy. The most expeditious processing of a suspect who pleaded not guilty and went to trial took 58 days from the incident to sentencing.

There were five suspects whose cases were not taken to trial within a year of the incident. By comparison, 20 were sentenced within six months of the murder. Even in the case of the suspect arrested 198 days after the incident, the entire proceeding was concluded within 270 days after the murder was committed. This suspect was arraigned the same day as his arrest, his preliminary hearing was 22 days later, and his trial was convened 39 days after the preliminary hearing. The trial lasted two days, after which the suspect was convicted. He was sentenced nine days after the verdict was entered, and he was transported to prison 11 days thereafter.

The speed with which these cases were processed not only speaks well of the judicial branch which heard the cases, but it also points to efficient police investigatory work which located the suspects very soon after the homicide. And it commends the prosecutor's staffs, too, for being trial-ready so promptly.

Certain characteristics which mark the various steps in the criminal justice process for Oklahoma murder suspects are now presented in greater detail.

Plea Bargaining

While there were a few occasions where prosecutors negotiated pleas with murder suspects, there were not many. When there was a bargain, it came about because of a weak evidentiary case or one suspect's testimony was needed against another suspect. As a general rule, however, plea bargaining is not likely, as the prosecutor may face monumental political consequences if he bargained out in an especially heinous case. It must be remembered that these trials are almost always highly visible and widely heralded by the media, and the conduct of the prosecutor is closely followed by the public. So the time from arrest to arraignment is that time when both prosecutors and defense attorneys go about assembling the material needed to put together their cases. Of course, there will be time for further case preparation all the way up to trial, which may be several months later.

Representation by Counsel

Many citizens believe that cop killers neither need nor deserve representation by counsel. They see these cases as open and shut and feel that counsel is unnecessary, a frill of our judicial process. Others sharply disagree, for where a person's life is the issue or the possibility of a life sentence exists, legal representation during the process to determine the suspect's guilt or innocence is imperative, as well as being constitutionally guaranteed by the Bill of Rights. The United States Supreme Court wholeheartedly agrees.

Of the 57 suspects who entered Oklahoma's criminal justice system, at least 55 were represented by counsel, either an attorney of his choosing or by a court-appointed lawyer. Information is too fuzzy to determine whether the other two were represented, although they probably were.

Counsel for the suspect serves to assure that the accused is afforded due process and to double-check police investigatory work, which must be impeccably done from the moment the call first breaks to trial. While the outcome of Oklahoma cases underscores the excellence of police criminal investigations and the pretrial preparation by the prosecution, by no means does it reflect a lack of ability on the part of defense counsel. The factual circumstances of almost all of the cases show that overwhelming evidence led to the suspects' conviction, not inept defense counsel. So attorneys for the defense should be welcome, and their role on behalf of their clients should be understood as the heartbeat of America's judicial system.

The belief that retained counsel was more effective than court-appointed counsel is not borne out in Oklahoma. Neither was the stereotype that a suspect charged with murdering a police officer is an impoverished, embattled criminal, unable to afford an attorney of his choice. The data reveal that about one of every three suspects was represented by retained, rather than court-appointed, counsel.

Bail

A widespread public viewpoint is that people suspected of killing police officers are too dangerous to be allowed on the streets. The amount of bail set by the court and the frequency with which bail is denied seems to reflect this. High bail and the suspect's inability to make it, or its denial, result in a long period of incarceration before trial for most police murder suspects. The purpose of bail is to insure that a suspect will be present for trial. Some of the points a judge takes into consideration deciding upon bail include the severity of the crime, the suspect's ties to the community, the danger the suspect poses to society if allowed bail, family and employment status, prior criminal history, parole or probation history, etc. The bail decision in cop killing cases may be laden with greater community feeling than the judgment in other types of cases. Cop killing is usually a high profile matter.

Once booked into jail, suspects are interested in the terms of their bail, or bond as it is called in some places. There are some offenses for which a judge is not required to set bail. Since a charge of murder in the first degree is one of these, it is not surprising that 43 of the 57 suspects were denied bail. Bail was set on 12 other suspects and two others, a 16-year-old male and a female, were released on their personal recognizance. Of the 12, only seven actually posted bail and were released pending hearings and trial.

The seven suspects who posted bail include two male suspects charged with manslaughter in the 1954 death of an Oklahoma City officer, both released on $5,000 bail. In an Ardmore case, a 69-year-old suspect was released on $500 bail—the lowest amount set for any of the suspects. He was in failing health when bail was set, a crucial factor in the judge's decision. Two other cop killers were disallowed bail because they were considered very dangerous. However, in these cases, bail was later allowed by the Court of Criminal Appeals, and it was posted, to the dismay of authorities.

Arrest to Arraignment

Once a suspect is arrested, due process requires that he be taken as soon as possible before a magistrate to be informed of the charges against him. This is termed an initial appearance. It is at this point that arrangements for counsel would be made, including the appointment of counsel if the suspect is unable to afford an attorney. Bail is usually set at this time, although the committing magistrate may not make a bail decision until the accused has counsel and has entered a plea to the charges. Finally, if the proceedings were going according to form, the judge sets a date for the arraignment.

The average time between arrest and arraignment was nearly two months. On the extremes, three suspects were arraigned one day after their arrest. The longest time between arrest and arraignment was for two suspects in a 1960 murder of an Ardmore officer—about 400 days each. A third suspect in that case spent 324 days in jail until he was finally arraigned. Today such a delay would almost certainly be grounds for reversible error, should there be a conviction at the subsequent trial. Significantly, the average time from arrest to arraignment, without including these three suspects' time, is but 28 days.

The Preliminary Hearing to Trial

Preliminary hearings were held on 41 suspects: eight others waived the privilege of the preliminary hearing and were bound over for trial. The data fail to disclose whether other suspects had such a hearing.

The preliminary hearing, which is a judicial hearing intended to determine if there is probable cause to bind a suspect over for trial on the charge, is not a constitutionally guaranteed right. It is an optional step in the judicial process which will allow the defense to discover the nature and extent of the state's evidence. It usually benefits the suspect's attorney in terms of trial preparation. The fact that 41 suspects opted to have a preliminary hearing seems to indicate the desire of the accused, through counsel, to get an early reading on chances for acquittal or to gauge the chances for a negotiated plea.

All 41 suspects were bound over. An average of 103 days elapsed between the preliminary hearings and the trial. In one case the trial began only five days after the preliminary hearing. The longest time from preliminary hearing to trial was nearly a year—322 days.

Dismissed Charges

That six suspects had charges against them dismissed seems unusual, since the dismissal of cop killing charges is not readily agreed to by a prosecuting attorney. When it happens, the dismissal order is almost surely based on unique circumstances. Furthermore, the prosecutor may be expected to quickly explain the dismissal, as in the Oklahoma cases. The six dismissals related below illustrate some typical but understandable circumstances which prompted charges being dropped.

Two suspects who were involved in a 1954 brawl which later involved two police officers had charges of manslaughter against them dismissed. An Oklahoma City officer and his partner were quelling an early morning family disturbance which had spilled out of a bar onto the center parkway strip on an arterial street. The victim was attempting to separate a husband and wife who were fighting, when he was pulled to the ground by the husband. The husband allegedly attempted to withdraw the officer's gun from its holster, which prompted his partner to draw his own gun. At this point in the melee, there was a gunshot. The slug tore into the officer's chest, killing him. The two suspects were arrested and charged, as it was thought that one of them had fired the gun which killed the officer. However, further investigation showed that the gun had discharged accidentally when the other officer used the firearm to strike one of the suspects.

Another dismissal was also in Oklahoma City. In this case, one suspect agreed to provide important evidence for the state during the trials of two other suspects. In return for this testimony, the suspect was granted immunity from prosecution and the murder charge against him was dismissed. The same circumstances brought about the dismissal of charges against one of two suspects in the 1982 murder of a Spencer officer. In neither of these cases was the person who gave testimony for the state the triggerman.

A mistrial in one case and a hung jury in the second are the reasons for the dismissal of charges against one suspect in the 1951 murder of a town marshal. In the sixth dismissal, a woman and her son were charged with murder in a 1969 case in Clinton. Eventually, the murder charge against the woman was dismissed after she had been through two trials which resulted in deadlocked juries. The likelihood that the prosecution could convince a jury beyond a reasonable doubt of her guilt precluded a third trial.

Length of the Trial

The longest of the 33 trials was 24 days. The suspect was found not guilty by reason of insanity and committed to a state mental institution. Two other trials, both of urban suspects, lasted 16 and 15 days, respectively. Seven of the 33 trials were started and finished on the same day. In two of the cases, the jury deliberated for only 30 minutes before returning a verdict! The average length of all trials for the 35-year span is 4.5 days.

Trials are definitely getting longer and more complicated. For example, the trials from 1950 through 1974 averaged 3.4 days duration. Trials in the last ten years averaged 11.2 days!

Several of the suspects, because of mistrials or higher court rulings, were tried more than once. A few suspects were tried for more than one murder.

Appeals and other postconviction maneuvers are not uncommon. These processes, though judicially time-consuming, are not difficult for a convicted prisoner to file, owing to a prisoner's access to free legal counsel and law libraries. Some become known as pretty good jailhouse lawyers! However, the record shows that Oklahoma cop killers have not had much luck with their postconviction gyrations.

Acquittals

There were two acquittals: One by reason of insanity; the other where the jury believed the theory that the suspect shot the officer in self-defense.

Time From Arrest to Sentencing

The criminal justice process grinds ahead slowly but deliberately in cop killings. Suspects spent an average of 167 days in jail from arrest to sentencing in the Oklahoma cases. While some cases were resolved very quickly, others lagged. For example, the three suspects in a 1960 murder in Ardmore remained in jail almost 14 months until sentenced. While a few suspects were languishing in jail between arrest and the trial outcome for a long time, no Oklahoma convictions were overturned on appeal on the basis of unreasonable delay.

Manslaughter Convictions

In homicide cases in Oklahoma, the judge must instruct the jury of the lesser-included offenses of homicide. These include second degree murder, first and second degree manslaughter, and involuntary manslaughter. The jury then must decide the degree of homicide appropriate to the evidence introduced. This may account for seven suspects being convicted of a less serious degree of homicide than the first degree murder charged.

Sentences of from five to 100 years were imposed on six killers following convictions for first degree manslaughter. A seventh person, charged with and convicted of second degree manslaughter, was sentenced to one year in jail and was fined $1,000. This suspect could have been sentenced to serve from two to four years in the Oklahoma State Penitentiary, but the evidence strongly suggested that he killed the officer unintentionally.

The six persons convicted of first degree manslaughter were originally charged with first degree murder. However, the complications of second and third trials, especially when the first trial had been reversed on appeal, may cause subsequent trials to result in conviction on lesser charges.

A tactical consideration sometimes prompts a district attorney to pursue a route assuring conviction on a manslaughter offense, rather than risking acquittal on a murder charge. A 1973 case where an officer was murdered by his prisoner is a good example of an appeals court opinion influencing the course of a second trial. In it, the suspect was initially convicted of murder by the jury and sentenced to life imprisonment. However, in the first trial, testimony from a psychiatrist with the State Department of Mental Health was introduced which concerned conversations between the suspect and the psychiatrist after the suspect had been committed to the hospital for observations, before trial but after arrest. The psychiatrist testified to these conversations which, in effect, were confessions of the crime. The Oklahoma Court of Criminal Appeals determined that this testimony was inadmissible at trial because it derived from a doctor-patient, confidential relationship. The conviction was reversed and the case was remanded with instructions that the psychiatrist's testimony may not be introduced in the second trial. The loss of this testimony forced the prosecutor in the second trial to seek a conviction for first degree manslaughter.

Sentences and the Death Penalty

Thirty-one of the 47 persons whose guilt was established were found guilty following trial by jury. Sixteen suspects pleaded guilty. Of the 47 persons — 45 men and two women — convicted or who pleaded guilty, the following sentences were assessed:

Death	7
Imprisonment for life	31
100 years	1
65 years	1
40 years	2
20 years	1
4 to 20 years	1
8 years	1
5 years	1
1 year in county jail and $1,000 fine	1
	47

Two men under life sentences or facing death for two murders are shown only once each on the charges, dispositions, and sentences in the tallies set out above and on pages 45 and 46.

With few exceptions, persons who murder police officers in Oklahoma pay a stiff price for their act. That 38 suspects have been sentenced either to life in prison or execution indicates public attitude toward this class of offender. The surprise is that so few suspects — only 7 — have been sentenced to death and only two executed! Both executions stemmed from murders committed well ahead of the July, 1972, **Furman vs. Georgia** United States Supreme Court decision which, for several years, effectively put capital punishment in limbo across the nation. These killers were put to death in 1956 and 1960, 445 and 609 days, respectively, after they murdered police.

PART II

WHAT TO DO ABOUT ATTACKS
ON POLICE

"COULD ANYTHING have been done to prevent their deaths?"
This recurring afterthought comes to mind in the wake of 2,129
police deaths since 1959. Nothing will bring life back to the victims, or
the loved ones to the survivors. But the murder of other police officers
can be prevented if sensible measures are implemented to reduce the
carnage.

Part II is devoted to reducing the slaughter. The ideas set out in the
pages which follow are not limited to Oklahoma, for the deaths of 54
Sooner State lawmen present a cross section, a mere microcosm, of what
haunts police in all 50 states, the territories, and other possessions.
Therefore, suggestions for improving and making innovations in training, procedures, and equipment which will lessen the likelihood of officers being slain can be applied everywhere.

No one knows for certain how to prevent assaults on America's
lawmen. Reasons, based on seasoned intuition, emerge after the fact;
veteran officers and nonpolice observers make objective professional
observations, and the resulting literature allows conjecture. But the
definitive study is yet to be done. Until more data and research appear, partly intuitive measures must be taken in the quest for solutions. Such an approach will not be free from four unfortunate
consequences.

First, police officers and suspects will continue to suffer injuries,
some fatal, owing to imperfect knowledge about what prompts people to
assault police. We do not yet know what the triggering variables are.
Lacking this information, the police are stymied in their attempts to develop all-inclusive countermeasures.

Second, as assaults on police continue, and if they escalate dramatically in number and gravity, the public may tacitly sanction oppressive police measures. This is contrary to the American tradition of liberty and safety within the framework of the law and must be resisted, as tempting as such measures may seem. The best way to forestall over-reaction is through public leadership which will not tolerate operational excesses. The judiciary can play a pivotal role by decisively affirming that excesses by or against the police will not be tolerated and that stiff, no-nonsense penalties will be meted out as appropriate.

Third, many think that the current tide of violence against the police is more than a specific attack against police authority. It is believed that this violence is directed toward bureaucracy in general by people frustrated by what they see as an unresponsive government. Legislative bodies, at all levels of government, must take persuasive measures, and quickly, to convince society that something is being done to alleviate the arbitrariness and impersonality of bureaucracy. Perhaps attacks on police officers will not drop until the quality of life and opportunity for many socioeconomic groups in this country is improved.

Fourth, the bulk of endeavors to reduce assaults should still be centered on taming the incident until research is directed toward potentially more productive areas.

In conclusion, many groups need to work together to create a comprehensive program to prevent assaults on police. This partnership includes the police and the people who train them, the United States Congress, state and local legislative bodies, professional organizations, police associations and unions, universities, private research foundations and civic groups, among others. Broadly, however, the range of casualty reduction measures should include action in the following areas: (1) preventing assaults by taking several steps within police forces; (2) improving training; (3) streamlining police procedures and upgrading operations manuals; (4) equipment improvement; (5) passing legislation; (6) implementing alcohol and other drug abuse reduction programs designed specifically for the violent offender; (7) reducing violence on television and in the movies; and (8) conducting applied research.

CHAPTER IV

PREVENTION FROM WITHIN
POLICE DEPARTMENTS

THERE ARE SEVERAL immediate measures which forces should take to make their officers safer. Some can be incorporated at little or no cost while others may require funds to cover costs of instructors and officer training time. Equipment costs will vary, depending on what type of gear is needed, its purchased price, and the quantity. The returns in officer safety may be dramatic, depending on the nature of the force and when, for example, tactical or procedural changes are made.

The following essays set forth areas within police forces that should be reviewed in order to enhance officer safety.

IMPROVING POLICE TRAINING

Simply stated, police officers should be trained to perform with efficiency, safety, and ease, and in accord with the law and departmental procedure. Thanks to the dramatic development and implementation of peace officer training commissions and mandatory minimum training standards laws in most states, almost all American police today are trained, but to varying levels of sophistication. **Training,** a very broad term, should be construed to mean much more than the training given in recruit school. It is essential that the term be understood to include the regular retraining of veteran personnel (called in-service training), the command training of supervisors, and executive level training, as well. Training should also embrace the field training given young officers by senior or master patrol personnel. Training goals should be to provide police at all levels with the skills they need to understand and execute complicated tasks.

Training is the single most important factor in preventing an officer from becoming a statistic. By far, the most important training is that which is geared to reducing officer carelessness and complacency. Periodic retraining will minimize these mind sets, and casualties will be reduced. But who knows how to do this effectively? Other training essential to casualty reduction includes simulations, attitude awareness, persuasion, personal defense, and classes on body language and con talk.

Overcoming Officer Carelessness and Complacency

For ages, police have fought criminals. But now, more than ever, police must fight carelessness, the greatest reason why police are killed. An effective, thorough training program is indispensable to combatting carelessness. Training is, as a matter of fact, a lifesaver. The need to train is ever-present in any size police or sheriff's department. But even the most thorough, realistic, and intensive training can be rendered ineffective when an officer has a complacent attitude. It is this state of mind that can lead officers to vulnerability and their own victimization. This mental attitude breeds carelessness, and such carelessness is what contributes to more police injuries and deaths than any other single factor.

Carelessness is often defined as human error. Though human error occurs in all occupations, with varying degrees of severity in the result, in few callings does it have the potential consequences it has in police work. A glitch in safety, an overlooked precaution, or a departure from proven patrol procedures can cost an officer his life. Of all officers murdered on duty, upwards of one-half were the principal contributors to their own slaying because they were careless.

The term "human error" has a negative connotation, as it denotes ineptness and lack of ability. Carelessness is central to "human error." While the level of skill or the amount of training and instruction will never completely negate the prospect of some human error, professionals have discovered that the prospect of human error is significantly reduced when more attention and time are given to instruction and training. Moreover, continuing training strengthens the lessons and habits learned in earlier training sessions, even years earlier.

So the point is this: If a police officer is to be safe from homicidal assault, he or she must be trained and regularly retrained, so that the chance for human error becomes minimal. Carelessness must be trained out of personnel, insofar as that can be done.

A positive attitude is the key to combatting carelessness. The officer's attitude is one side of what experts refer to as the survival triangle, the other two sides being tactics and shooting skills. For example, certain types of calls may become routine in the officer's mind, like the couple which is frequently fighting and the police are summoned. Such family disturbances are resolved when the principals have finally calmed down and been separated, which usually isn't too hard to accomplish. At the same time, data show that more police are murdered while intervening in these types of calls than any other. This suggests carelessness; the rote handling of chronic calls. The importance of a positive attitude must be drilled in the officer's mind, for if he or she becomes careless, trouble is sure to follow in the form of serious injury or death.

While the toll is high, by no means is the murder of every police officer a product of officer carelessness. For example, there are those instances where a sniper's bullet or other unprovoked sudden attack kills a conscientious, highly perceptive officer. Those deaths are virtually unavoidable. On the other hand, some officers murdered in the line of duty were careless as they went about their work, though they certainly were not unconcerned about their own life. In the incidents where an officer's misjudgement is contributory to his own murder, the mistake is frequently due to carelessness. Such carelessness results in a diminished awareness and perception of the dangers inherent in patrol situations.

Complacency plagues even the most experienced officers at some time during their careers. It is a product of boredom, which is literally a mental narcotic so often borne of patrolling. Patrolling, as any police officer knows, most of the time is essentially routine. In reality, it bears little resemblance to how it is portrayed on television where, in an hour, incidents an officer may face but a few times in a career, if ever, happen. Action on patrol normally doesn't provide the second-by-second excitement worthy of a Hollywood epic. Actually, most patrol time is spent handling noncrime fighting activities. Hence, at times, patrol can be very monotonous.

The complacency syndrome has not escaped detection and comment by experts. For example, former FBI Director Clarence M. Kelley addressed this point:

"Complacency is always a dangerous foe. For a law enforcement officer, it can be a deadly enemy.

. . . [An officer] must constantly remind himself that there is nothing routine in law enforcement duty. He cannot shirk that duty even when it — as it frequently does — propels him suddenly and without warning into the jaws of grave human conflict. At these dangerous times, an officer's only companion is his alertness. . . . It is likely that there will always be ambush assassins, frenzied terrorists, ruthless killers, desperate felons, and emotionally overwrought persons to threaten the lives of law enforcement officers. Our complacency, however, must never be permitted to aid this perilous band of police killers."

Kelley's message is clear: Officers must be constantly alert. But alertness is more than just officer awareness of the potential danger of a situation: it encompasses officer perception of how he will be accepted and what his role is in a given situation and his ability to adjust to that given circumstance.

Former Director Kelley is not the only FBI leader to see complacency as a condition which may be the direct road to disaster. Earlier, the Bureau's first director, J. Edgar Hoover, wrote that:

"The tragic total of policemen slain last year brings out crucial points that all officers should remember: (1) complacency is most dangerous, and (2) there is no such thing as a 'routine' arrest."

In summary, no one enjoys being lectured or told what to do. Police officers in this sense are like all other human beings. That is why the awareness factor in police work needs to be clearly highlighted and emphasized in police recruit training. Recruits expect to be told what to do. However, instruction needs to be given in a relevant way, so the lessons taught may be retained throughout the officers' service. Complacency and carelessness sometimes accompany longevity in a profession. Therefore, regular in-service sessions for police officers are essential, too. These future instructional blocks should reemphasize the fundamental safety principles learned during initial instruction.

Simulation Training

Traditional classroom instructional methods may often be inappropriate for both recruit and in-service police training. While suitable for the teaching of law, sociology, and other dry subjects, hands-on training is more likely to catch and hold the trainees' attention and to be retained by the trainees. Hands-on training will also allow veteran police instructors, who may not be at their best in the classroom, to effectively transfer their professionalism during several practical exercises.

Officers are victimized in some of the most congested places imaginable — kitchens, living or family rooms, restaurants, pool halls! Where there is an attack with a gun, it is almost certain to come at a range of ten or fewer feet. Non-firearm attacks almost always occur in closer quarters, too, though rock and bottle tossing incidents are the most notable exceptions. The scene usually includes chairs, tables, lamps, stools, dishes, and ashtrays, all of which are found in the kitchen or living room, the frequent locale of the domestic quarrel. Parking meters, trees, garbage cans, curbstones, and so forth, mark street scenes. In a car, the steering wheel may be used as an effective means in pinning the officer as he attempts to ward of a sudden attack by a prisoner whom he is transporting to jail or the mental hospital.

It makes good sense for trainers to bring the instrumentalities of the scene, like the steering wheel, the sidewalk, bar stools, pool tables, ashtrays, and even the kitchen sink, into the classroom to simulate the field conditions under which officers must ward off varying forms of attack. In simulated settings, the student will face the situation as he is likely to find it, instead of the one-dimensional experience of learning personal defense in the antiseptic setting of an expansive gymnasium, free of hazards and obstructions. Trainers may readily procure old auto cabs and set up other mock conditions of combat to better simulate actual field incidents. Such simulated settings are limited only by the trainer's imagination (and maybe his budget!). The simulated setting may even include making a facsimile street!

Simulation training has been upgraded immeasurably, thanks to audiovisual equipment which enables the training staff to introduce a high degree of realism and stress in whatever exercise trainees are handling. Experts have combined various multimedia techniques so that a microprocessor can be programmed to completely control the settings to which an officer is exposed. These settings, of course, can be varied to make scenarios more or less intensive, depending on the competence level of a trainee or class. Equipment which allows a wide range of flexibility and adaptability to be brought into the classroom is of extraordinary value in enhancing officer training.

Simulation training is one mode of instilling awareness and perception of the dangers of particular types of police-citizen encounters. This method involves police academy instructors and students as actors in a typical police-citizen encounter, such as a traffic stop. It offers cadets practical, realistic learning experiences. Simulation exercises have been made easier, thanks to the introduction of role-playing techniques augmented by appropriate films.

Several forces have adopted a program of hands-on instruction. Incorporating role-playing techniques, situations are created on the street which best simulate the actual conditions officers will confront while performing their assignments. Moreover, such a program can be especially helpful when it is actually given on the street. Fully videotaped, a traffic accident is simulated at a normal intersection and a student officer is required to handle the situation, including directing the traffic. At the end of each training session a critique should be held, with both the training center staff and the actors who participated offering constructive criticism. During such sessions, instructors should set out correct answers to questions regarding procedures raised by the student officers. Fights, traffic stops, and citizen encounters could take place outside, too. Family calls and other disturbances may be simulated indoors in appropriately adorned rooms.

Those departments that are equipped to provide trainees with videotaped instant replays of simulated encounters enhance their training opportunities. This method, a very popular one, points out errors while the class watches itself on the screen—sometimes with understandable amusement! Viewing a televised picture, trainee officers see firsthand the importance of proper, self-protectionary police procedures. Whatever entertainment or humor is seen may be valuable to buttress the grim career-long lesson to be learned. Additionally, the attention of the trainee is more completely captured when he is observing himself on the screen, and therefore the lessons learned are more likely to be internalized and remembered throughout a career.

Dozens of film companies, directing their efforts at presenting simulated situations, have produced short film clips of various stress situations. Done authentically, films show the inherent violent explosiveness of all sorts of transactions, and set out the appropriate police responses. Trainees can learn by seeing dozens of situations, rather than merely being told about them. The lessons taught by books and the experiences recounted by seasoned officers and trainees will be reinforced by the use of training films. The value of reinforcement in education should not be overlooked or minimized.

A very popular training film, titled "Shoot-Don't Shoot," puts officers in simulated situations with only a split second in which to decide whether or not to fire at a suspect who confronts them on the screen. The film offers on-screen interactions with the viewing police personnel. The film is primarily devised to help teach officers when and when not to use their firearms. However, it is useful as a realistic training device that forces the student police officer to interact with a common, hazardous situation. The film also offers untold instructional advantages to the officer on how to protect his own life in a dangerous situation.

Another film "Deadly Force Decisions," helps officers learn to make a reasoned shoot-don't shoot decision quickly, under stress, and before they must face the true test on the street. The 31-minute film features 12 individual episodes, with 30 key decision junctures for trainees based on actual street confrontations. Films such as "Shoot-Don't Shoot" and "Deadly Force Decisions" underscore the fact that officers must always be alert, disciplined and trained in matters of fatal force, and sensitive to the consequences of split-second decisions which are forced upon them. Such simulation training is of extraordinary value.

Officers are not always cognizant of the possible danger inherent in a stress call, such as domestic or other disturbance calls. The national figures for police officers killed while responding to this class of incident testify to this fact. From 1965 through 1984, 310 officers were murdered while responding to disturbance calls. This represents 16.2 percent of the 1,918 U.S. police murdered over that time span. Training films, followed by simulated circumstances which are videotaped and then discussed, have made and kept police constantly aware of the sudden dangers involved in handling disturbance situations and thereby reduced the tendency of the officer to fall prey to carelessness and complacency.

Attitude Awareness Classes

Today, instruction in psychology, sociology, and human relations is given in many, but not all, police department academies. At the very minimum, all law enforcement officers should receive an introductory academy course in these behavioral sciences. Recognizing others' attitudes towards police and the likelihood of certain behavior is as important to officers as the lifesaving instruction offered at the police academy level. Awareness classes, then, can be viewed as another step in making the law enforcement officer totally aware of the inherent dangers found in this profession.

Effective instruction in this subject should be continued throughout each officer's career. Aside from the academy instruction, all officers would benefit by taking training seminars conducted by psychologists, psychiatrists, sociologists, and criminologists, perhaps from a nearby college. These seminars would draw a group of police together, with a behavioral scientist as their discussion leader. Sessions should be lively, especially if officers have completed pertinent reading assignments in preparation for their classes. Discussion, ideally, would center on views of the police officer by the citizen in trouble, and how officers perceive their own roles. In this atmosphere, outside ideas, criticisms, praise, and recommendations would be most beneficial to officers. Too often the police themselves only see one side to a situation, ignoring attitudes present in the citizen. Yet perception of citizen's attitudes helps an officer to predict aggressive, violent behavior.

The exact structure and content of the seminars, academy courses, and other instructional methods should be at the discretion of the local training officer but within the context of what the department perceives as its need for training of this sort. Every effort to bring current behavioral science knowledge and working police operatives together should be encouraged. There is ample room for creativity and experimentation. Why not invite psychologists, sociologists, and psychiatrists to ride along with patrol officers? These professionals could get a "no-holds-barred" perspective of violence and social conflict, a perspective very real to police. It could also mean that as police and professionals chat while on patrol, officers get an enhanced understanding of the sociopsychological framework which underlies observable human behavior.

Attitude awareness training should be aimed at attacking negative attitudes and stereotypes that come through unawareness and misinformation often common to policing. Sessions should aim to make officers more aware of the attitudes and needs within their community. By sensitizing officers to the cultural differences among groups with which they regularly work, many of the interpretive judgements which police unknowingly make may be prevented. If so, this should ease racial, cultural, and socioeconomic tension, antagonism, and suspicion. Such awareness can also contribute to officer safety when personnel have a better understanding of cultural mores.

Persuasion and Personal Defense Training

The best police "come-along" is the spoken word! There is none more effective, and there never will be. Hence, police must be afforded as much training in the art of persuasion as a department's curriculum allows.

Police work is work with the spoken word. Expressed in different terms, police work is made infinitely more difficult without the spoken word or effective verbal and nonverbal communication. Often, police work includes persuading an individual or a group to do something they aren't eager to do. Effective persuasion techniques can bring about dramatic successes when delivered convincingly, with authority, but yet with a virtual velvet tongue. Few classes of work find the need for persuasion more often or in more important circumstances than police.

It's not so much the message itself as how that message is delivered that moves people either positively or negatively. Such considerations include both verbal and nonverbal communications skills, such as word usage, voice strength and tone, timing, inflection, eye contact, and other aspects of body language, all of which bear heavily on the success of a message. So does the setting in which the message is delivered, although officers cannot always control this aspect.

Whatever decision an officer reaches to resolve a problem, he must act decisively. This is true whether the incident is one dealing with drunken or mentally disturbed persons, or one dealing with persons who are angry or openly hostile. Part of police training must underscore the fact that officers, by their very actions or merely their presence, may trigger citizens to violent, hostile, or aggressive behavior against police. Officers must realize that the words they use, their demeanor in speakng to a suspect, and their overall bearing can be decisive factors in determining the direction a police-citizen contact may take. If a contact goes poorly, an assault may ensue. The *FBI Law Enforcement Bulletin* noted that for an officer's own protection, he should become familiar with antagonistic words and types of overt conduct that are likely to incite an individual to great violence, and, of course, should avoid such words or conduct:

". . . The police officer must carefully maintain his instrument—speech. He should strive to be as precise with the word as the surgeon is with the scalpel since his operations can also be serious and delicate."

Even the simple utterance, "You're under arrest," might touch off a sudden savage burst of violence in a suspect. So officers must be aware of the possibility of that happening. Their awareness must, of course, come from training—and retraining.

In summary, each law enforcement officer must clearly realize the variety of ways in which he may appear to other persons. His presence is a symbol of authority. To many, this is comforting. To some, unfortunately, it provokes anxiety and fear. This gamut of emotions spells danger for a law enforcement officer.

Persuasion training should be taught to an extent well beyond that which it is today. It could readily be worked into that portion of training which deals with the mechanics of arrest, as this is where it will prove of extraordinary value and help reduce resistance to officers.

Persuasion is only one of many tools, tactics, and techniques available to officers in the performance of their duties. Not every tool, tactic, and technique will be used in every incident. Sometimes one, sometimes another, and most often a combination of several skills will be required.

Another tool is personal defense. Officers must continue to be trained, and regularly retrained, in unarmed personal defense, including, but not limited to, baton or billy stick exercises. There are many acceptable techniques and training publications dealing with such training.

However, a critical element which is often overlooked is the training of officers to defend themselves as individuals but also to defend themselves while working in teams of two or three, as a group, and in defense of one another. Accordingly, academy training in personal defense should not only feature basic holds, strokes, and parries, but train officers to work in tandem, as a team, in order to overcome attacks. These modules should feature two officers vs. three suspect tactics, two-on-two encounters, and so forth, to be practical. And these sessions should include conflicts in cluttered settings, such as rooms, booking facilities, elevators, auto interiors, and so forth. Clutter-free gymnasium facilities don't fill the bill. Let's train officers in the object-filled surroundings in which they will be utilizing these skills at some suddenly arising, later occasion.

Reading Body Language

Making the decision to arrest is one thing; effecting it peacefully is another. Voice and bearing, the most effective police "come-alongs," are crucial to controlling the suspect. There is an additional element to keeping the peace and assuring safety which must be better understood by police. That element is learning to read the body language of every contact, be it victim, witness, complainant, or suspect.

Social scientists and doctors have been refining intriguing concepts stemming from psychology and physiology. These concepts describe human behavior police often encounter. Writers such as Julius Fast in **Body Language**,[1] and Robert Ardrey in **The Territorial Imperative**,[2]

---

[1] Julius Fast, **Body Language**, New York, Pocket Books, 1970.
[2] Robert Ardrey, **Territorial Imperative**. New York, Antheneum Press, 1966.

have done the police a vast, though as yet not widely heralded, service by setting out the science of kinesics. Kinesics deals with physical signals—the body language—humans send out. By studying these concepts, police may pick up subtler, earlier warning of potential attacks on themselves.

These books explain that a person's body "talks." An alert observer may "hear," read, sense, or interpret what comes next by observing what the person is "saying" by means of nonverbal communication. One's body language, coupled with verbal outpourings, evident alcohol intake, the physical surroundings, etc., is a virtual road map which allows an officer to anticipate near-range behavior. Modern police training must include a significant module to help officers read suspects' body language, as well as to control their own. In a way, reading body language is an exercise in intellectual judo!

Here is an example of body language familiar to every lawman. An officer tells a suspect that he is under arrest, only to be cursed and verbally abused. Annoyed, the officer places his hand on the suspect, pressing the arrest, and easing the suspect toward the police car and jail. Quick as a wink, in response to pressure the officer has applied with his hand, the suspect swings on the officer.

The suspect is responding violently to an invasion of his territorial space. Violence follows, perhaps prolonged and leading to intense resistance. The predictability of this transaction should be understood by every officer. Alternative methods for getting this suspect to jail without a fight should be discussed. The more completely officers understand body language, or kinesics, and the more accurately they translate it into intellectual judo, the more likely it is that they will take the necessary countermeasures that will prevent assaults upon themselves.

Con Talk, Games, and Tattoos

Convicts in penitentiaries have their own type of speech—a special jargon used in their world. It can be speech by words or tattoos, or perhaps conveyed by other means. Cons play games, too, in order to control the behavior of institutional staff and fellow inmates.

Since most felons do county or municipal lock-up time awaiting trial, or are in the county jail on a reduced charge, inmates on these levels also use con talk, as well as tattoo themselves. Such communication, to the untutored ear or eye, is almost foreign, and therefore "unheard". Analyze the following bit of conversation between two cons: "We kicked in, blasted the pete, glommed on the bread, and took off like a shot-at-cat.

We didn't get a rumble." Translated, this means "We broke in, blew open the safe, took the money, and left as fast as we could. We didn't have any trouble."

Knowledge of such lingo is indispensable to the prison guard or county jailer. Prisoners, by using this slang, could hatch escape plans, plot murders, and plan other criminal activities merely by communicating verbally with the other inmates. Cons often use their jargon as a means to test guards, too. Guards, if acquainted with the jive talk, could respond with a suitable put-down or tell the cons to knock off the game playing. In any event, the hazard to corrections officials is evident.

Corrections officials are not the only people who are vulnerable when this jargon is spoken but not understood. Police officers, too, frequently have contact with former felons. Early recognition of con talk and tattoos may lead the officer to immediately identify the person as a con, or at least a person who has had earlier experience with the juvenile or criminal justice system. If so, the officer can take added precautions, as the setting seems to dictate. Additionally, if police better understood what the ex-con was saying or what tattoos meant, officers might be able to go about their work with a minimum of risk. In addition to perhaps detecting an early attack on themselves, officers might put themselves closer to the scene where former prisoners assemble by understanding con talk, tattoos, and games.

One way to help police learn con talk would be to have someone at the state penitentiary serve as a lexicographer. This person, skilled in English slang "jargonese," would keep prison staff, as well as police across each state, up to date on the current context and meaning of ever-changing con talk. The same skill is needed from persons familiar with the latest in tattoos and games. Periodic rap sessions and training bulletins, and even scheduled broadcasts across each state on educational television, would be the central means of information dissemination.

It is important that jail and prison personnel know all they can about how the games cons play work. Staff should learn how to recognize, stop, and prevent games which are nothing but one form of manipulation. Employees should recognize the steps in the setup and decide which tactics are most suited to sidetracking the ploys.

About tattoos: Tattoos, often common among felons, may convey a language all their own, too. For example, about 25,000 of the 125,000 refugees who flooded the United States in the early 1980s from the Cuban port of Mariel were hardened criminals, purposely sent to America by Fidel Castro. Many of these thugs bear tattoos on various parts of their bodies. Therefore, lawmen should be specially alert when tattoos are found on the web of the hand, between the thumb and index finger, especially of the left hand. These are Cuban government incarceration tattoos and brand the wearer as among the baddest of the bad, a designation proudly worn by the bearer.

The Marielitas have no corner on tattooing as a form of communication. Outlaw motorcycle gang members, other gangs in prison, and some military units have adorned themselves in unique ways, signifying membership or conveying messages. Police should be alert to these signs, too.

Early-Identifying Cop Fighters

Operationally, a force's administration may take a page from the Internal Revenue Service's bag of tricks. In 1985, the IRS implemented a system whereby key taxpayer files were marked with "PDT," a designation which identified someone as a "potentially dangerous taxpayer." A PDT notation is intended to early-warn agents and employees that should a "PDT" come to an IRS office or if a field contact must be made, the person has on earlier occasions used weapons or animals to threaten or intimidate an employee or has specifically threatened bodily harm. The designation may also be made for someone who has a record of violent behavior or who is shown to be an active member of a group advocating violence against the IRS or who has threatened or assaulted employees of other federal, state or local agencies. A program similar to the dangerous taxpayer identification program may be devised and built into a computer-based system by an enterprising police force in an effort to early-warn its field personnel about persons who have a local history of cop fighting.

THE ADMINISTRATION HAS A ROLE

The everyday management decisions of a force fall to the ranking personnel. These persons are responsible for implementing programs and establishing policies regarding recruitment, training and procedures which bear greatly on the safety of police officers. Ranking personnel, then, must be certain that operations or procedures manuals are up to date, and that supervision is provided throughout the force irrespective of time and place. It is also incumbent upon administrators to recognize the significance of the first level supervisor and take steps to shore up these critical persons who have the toughest job on the force. The executive suite can also set out some realistic guidelines governing off shift jobs for police. It may also consider the appropriateness of implementing an auxiliary, or reserve police officer program, and set out some incentives to assure that cops keep a high level of physical fitness, too.

Procedures Manuals

Adequate, up to date, utilitarian procedures manuals are essential to successful police field procedures. The written guidelines should be simple, clearly written, concise, complete, drafted in positive rather than negative language, divided into appropriate sections and indexed. Police administrators should prepare and make available to the force specific procedural guidelines, covering about every circumstance which may be anticipated with some degree of regularity within their jurisdiction. For example, national guidelines or state training curricula may apply to most common situations, but specific guidelines should be drafted to cover a majority of possible stress situations which physically threaten an officer. A few forces have developed superior operational manuals. Of course, procedures manuals need regular updating and enlarging, as dangerous street strategies surface.

Some forces adapt certain sections of procedures manuals into training bulletins which are reviewed at roll call sessions, with each officer getting a copy. Such a training bulletin is usually a synthesis of many, many pages in a procedural manual and is exactly the type of instructional material which is needed to help officers translate the procedures manual to a street situation. It should enable officers to confront any number of trying circumstances with a minimum of danger. Without the benefit of specific procedures and training information, situations may escalate into violence and endanger officers.

Offering Variety on Patrol

Police patrol work, the mainstay of American law enforcement, is often unpleasant. There is not much humor, although on some occasions police are able to express sympathy and give nonphysical aid to people. Although not often aggressive, citizens are also not usually positive and affectionate toward the police.

There may be some nominally changed modes of police patrol, especially in larger cities. Changing the time and substituting specific crime fighting activities into each patrol duty, and allowing officers to train in other specialities are some of the methods administrators have employed in order to stem complacency and apathy in patrol personnel. Whatever happens—if anything, be it SWAT teams, helicopters, roles as hostage negotiators, canine handlers, emergency medical technicians, ready reserves, or any other roles—police supervisors should keep in mind that the monotony of routine patrol can lead to complacency—a perhaps fatal attitude for a police officer to have.

Psychologists Daniel Cruse and Jesse Rubin conducted research in Miami, Florida, which was prompted by deteriorating police-citizen relationships and mounting violence in that city. In their study, **Determinants of Police Behavior,** the two psychologists, recognizing the fact that police get bored, recommended that police recruits be trained in a sub-speciality:

> "Because of the role conflict inherent in policing today, as well as the serious deleterious effects of the inactivity and boredom, it is recommended that each cadet be trained in a sub-speciality, such as emergency medical care, settling minor civil disturbances, handling of alcoholics and/or drug addicts. During his regular patrol, he would also be expected to function in wide areas of the city as a specialist. The generalist-specialist would be kept more busy and less susceptible to boredom. Training toward being a generalist-specialist as an integral part of the policeman's identity should be started in cadet school."

In several ways, perhaps the patrol officer's vigilance will increase with the rigors of the police task. An officer who knows his job, appreciates the dangers involved, and realizes the value of his particular task, will be less apt to drift into complacency and hence be less likely to be an attack victim.

Effective Supervision

If training programs are to be effective and increase safety, then constructive supervision and positive discipline are essential in a police force. For example, if an officer's bad habits, once detected, go uncorrected, they may become ingrained, destroying benefits from otherwise effective training programs.

Discipline is essential in police work as in any organization. However, police personnel share a common bond and are a closely knit group, similar to soldiers in combat. Mutual feelings and comradeship are beneficial, but may also wreak havoc with a force's disciplinary system. No officer likes to see a fellow officer reprimanded for mishandling a boring, tedious aspect of patrol, especially if he or she would probably have done the same thing under the same circumstances.

The solution to this very complex aspect of interpersonal relations rests with the supervisor. First, the problem must be detected. Once aware of the situation, be it an infraction, a sloppy habit or other problem, the supervisor must react to it by drawing from the variety of appropriate means at his disposal, surely on a constructive basis for initial instances. However, the supervisor must not permit a sense of empathy for any officer to influence the exercise of supervisory responsibilities. To do so fosters carelessness and complacency — two of the greatest dangers to police officers. Effective discipline will enhance training and its unduring effect. To follow the logical conclusion one step further, good training makes for fewer victim officers.

Let's recognize the most important member of any police force: the first level supervisor! These are persons who represent officers to management, and management (and all sorts of administrative fiats) to officers. These are the persons who, more than any others, are in the middle of whatever is happening. First level supervisors must be geniuses of sorts to do an effective job! Not surprisingly, everyone's safety is related to the quality, dedication and adequate numbers of first level field supervisors, irrespective of their division. These persons, usually called sergeants, are the most important people on the force, for if they are careless, sloppy, unmotivated, not playing their role and are really just "promoted police officers" the vitality of the force will suffer, as will discipline, direction and control. Poor quality first level supervisors almost surely means there is no prospect that officers will perform their work in accordance with procedures, policy and guidelines. Conversely, caring, motivated and "in touch" first level supervisors who have their fingers on the troops' pulse and who assume a dynamic leadership role by insisting upon safe and positive performance among subordinate personnel bring a level of excellence to a force that is a joy to behold.

The Officer With Two Jobs

Moonlighting has been attacked by supervisors in almost all callings as poor practice. The usual, understandable criticism is that a person can't hold down two jobs and contribute his best efforts to each. In police work, moonlighting is discouraged, or even prohibited, for this reason, and also because it may contribute to the likelihood of an officer failing to be alert. While all of these evils exist, the main reason officers moonlight is because of low police salaries, an issue which urgently begs for solution. Bodies responsible for appropriations must be pressured to meet the financial levels police deserve.

In the meantime, in police work, an officer who has moonlighted within hours of reporting for duty can be expected to be tired, functioning at less than maximum efficiency and more importantly less than alert. Those who are slated to moonlight after their police duty tour are under pressure, too, for they may feel they must physically save themselves, thus affecting their police work and perhaps the safety of their associates. Once again, alertness may suffer. Yet alertness is the keynote of police efficiency and survival. The fact that off-shift jobs debilitate officers prompted the late FBI Director Hoover to stridently deplore moonlighting:

"Law enforcement is highly exacting work. It demands mental and physical alertness, single-mindedness, dedication, and enthusiasm for effective performance. To fully discharge his responsibilities and do a creditable job, an officer should devote all his energy to his enforcement duties. Unfortunately, many cannot do this. They are required to "moonlight" in order to give their families a decent standard of living."

Director Hoover closed by declaring that: "All communities should pay policemen suitable wages and let moonlighting pass from the scene."

Controlling moonlighting is not easy to do. Many forces have tried to limit an officer's moonlighting to no more than four hours each day, and preferably less, believing that if an officer works more than four hours, he cannot possibly be mentally prepared to hit the street at the top of either his physical or mental game. Others have limited moonlighting to a maximum of 20 hours a week. Some have specified certain types of work officers cannot do while off shift. Most forces have obliged moonlighting officers to secure approval in writing for their role before being allowed to work off shift.

The moonlighting problem nags law enforcement agencies and officers alike, and there is no easy solution. But steps should be taken by each department where moonlighting continues to be a problem either to get pay raises or find ways to limit the number of off-shift hours worked. Or both.

The added monthly income will be meaningless if the second job induced a lapse in an officer's mental alertness or so debilitated his physical ability which lead to a violent homicidal assault against him. The monetary advantages of a moonlighting job need to be weighed carefully against the disastrous, tragic results that could befall an officer during a duty tour.

Auxiliary Police

Many forces have a part-time, trained auxiliary police unit to relieve the regular police of certain time-consuming, routine, noncrime fighting activities, which can be effectively handled by para-professional or volunteer persons. An auxiliary force, properly trained and equipped which understands police work, can be a safety increment for regular personnel.

There is a growing and impressive precedent for voluntary auxiliary police units. Some of our largest forces have thousands of trained auxiliary police. They are uniformed, equipped with handcuffs, nightsticks and walkie-talkies, yet do not carry guns. Their primary mission is not to apprehend criminals but to assist the public in many and varied routine matters and to look out for potential criminal activity, and, when seen, to report it. The auxiliaries, in essence, are the skilled eyes and ears of the public, alert to the characteristics of potential trouble and how it might be headed off. Moreover, when regular police are called to a suspicious circumstance reported by the auxiliaries, they may go in with an idea of what's brewing, indeed forewarned of potentially ugly conditions.

A host of departments have added another group of enthusiastic volunteers to help with police work. This body is the trained explorer scouts, young men and women whose work has helped cut down on the workload of regular police, hence saving money and enhancing officer safety.

Freeing regular police of complacency-inducing activities, which might contribute to an officer's vulnerability at a critical time, is helpful. So is having a group of extra eyes and ears on the street. There are many virtues to implementing auxiliary police and explorer scout programs in forces which do not now have them.

Physical Fitness Programs

Many police personnel eat the wrong food, are overweight, smoke too much, drink too much coffee and don't get enough physical exercise. Occupational hazards? These conditions need not be since each officer, for the most part, has dominion and control over whether or not to smoke, what to eat and drink, as well as exercising. It's simply that many people are insufficiently disciplined and lack the personal will to translate one's resolve into action.

Officers who are not in good physical condition endanger not only their own lives but those of other police. Out-of-shape people lose some of their physical and mental keenness in crisis situations, too. The fact that police work and crisis management are not strange bedfellows is internationally known.

Persons in other than top physical shape are more subject to being injured on the job. They are also more likely to be cut down by heart attacks, high blood pressure and circulatory diseases. There is a greater chance that these officers will suffer a back injury, too, than are well conditioned personnel.

Not many police forces have implemented any kind of physical fitness training or weight maintenance programs. Moreover, very few forces have offered a reward or incentive program for officers who keep themselves trim. Research discloses that prison inmates, as a group, are in better physical fitness than police and have greater endurance! This is alarming, if not insulting, and should be redressed.

Good physical fitness is good personal business. It's where staying free of injury begins. Departments should insist upon fitness for all personnel.

IMPROVING POLICE
OPERATIONAL PROCEDURES

Operations constitute the fieldwork of a police department and should produce maximum efficiency with the least expense and effort. Operations, which are field procedures performed by uniformed and detective personnel, are directed toward achieving an organization's purpose. In law enforcement these are the services rendered to the public — patrol, traffic regulation, crime prevention and investigation, and so forth. That the administration should strive for effectiveness in the best fashion involving the least cost and effort, is obvious.

Uniformed police officers perform almost all of the basic police tasks, carrying out various procedures spanning the entire range of police services. A police force, therefore, is really no better than its uniformed personnel. The existence of an alert, adequately equipped, well supervised and properly trained patrol force is the best known deterrent to criminal activity. Moreover, citizens judge the police, and extend or withhold their support and cooperation on the basis of the appearance, attitude and conduct of the personnel in uniform. So an effective police program, therefore, depends to a great extent upon how well the force executed basic police procedures. The safety of personnel is related to effective field procedures, too.

The passage of time has seen several forces make some changes in their traditional police field procedures. Over the past ten years, many forces have devised and implemented a variety of directed patrol programs which place uniformed personnel in more of a proactive than reactive mode. These include such strategies as team policing, integrated criminal apprehension programs and split force patrols. Programs such as these try to systematically target crime and other negative conditions within sectors in a locale which earlier experience shows warrants greater-than-usual police coverage.

By no means should administrators or officers be deceived by these programs as danger still lurks for personnel involved in their execution! So while strategies or approaches may have been modified from more traditional ones, there is still ample opportunity for police to be attacked.

Officer Field Survival

An officer is cruising down a deserted street in a plainly marked police car in a large city. Suddenly, shots ring out targeting the car. What does the officer do?

Normal human behavior and police procedures call for the officer to remove himself from the line of fire. Then the officer must quickly assess the situation, determining the number and position of the assailants insofar as this can be done. This information must be radioed at once to headquarters together with a request for immediate assistance. Surprisingly, many departments provide no written guidelines for just such an event, although such an incident was covered during the officer's initial training. However, such knowledge usually fades with time.

Still other departments have simulated these exact conditions during training, and have developed a checklist as well as field procedures. The fact that such incidents occur infrequently is not a valid reason for failing to prepare personnel for such an ugly eventuality. When an officer's life is on the line, administrative difficulties and field probabilities should not enter the picture. An officer under fire must react instinctively and take the evasive measures which utilize his previous training. Any reaction, other than a virtually instinctive one, may mean another dead cop.

There are some impressive training programs for these circumstances. One seeks to minimize police exposure to assaults, and, if there is an assault, sets out the manner by which officers may defend themselves. Firing positions that decrease the amount of exposed body bulk, while maintaining the ability to return fire, are taught; protective seating positions in a car are shown; and procedures which are reactionary to ambushes are also part of the instruction.

These ideas are not new; they are an impressive compilation of existing police defensive tactics drawn together and presented very logically as a training module. The most important concept in a training module of this sort is this: officers under stress who must make quick, life-saving decisions will revert to techniques ingrained in their earlier training. Hence one's early training, or conditioning, is highly relevant to how an officer responds to sudden life-threatening pressure.

Another important survival consideration calls for officers on routine patrol to be ever alert to just where they are in relation to their field surroundings. Also, they should be alert to whomever may be encountered in certain places, and appreciate the mental stresses which may be nagging people at specific locales. For example, officers should know the location of residences for abused and battered women and children. Should there be reports of disturbances there, or men are seen lurking nearby, responding officers may anticipate encountering people under immense psychological stress who may react aggressively to police with little or no provocation. In fact, attacks without warning may be more likely in this setting than in many others.

Pierce R. Brooks, homicide detective in Joseph Wambaugh's nonfiction best-seller, **The Onion Field,** devised an impressive checklist for police officer field survival. He included the checklist in his officer survival book, **Officer Down, Code 3 . . . .**[3] The list, very useful because it hits hard at officers' bad practices, is set out below.

1. Bad attitude
2. Sleepy or asleep on duty
3. Taking a bad position
4. Missing the danger signs
5. Failure to watch hands
6. Poor or no search
7. Relaxing too soon
8. Improper use of handcuffs
9. Poor care and use of weapons
10. Tombstone courage

---

[3]Pierce R. Brooks, **Officer Down, Code 3 . . .**, Schiller Park, Illinois, Motorola Teleprograms, Inc., 1975.

In addition to the survival checklist and his book, Brooks has prepared a course entitled, "Police Officer Field Survival." This course is
given on request to various law enforcement groups around the country.
The instruction is keyed to six classic cases which highlight primary factors in the fatal shootings of police officers. After enlisting the help of a
panel of internationally recognized homicide investigators, Brooks indexed nine elements which contribute to officer victimization. Brooks
lists sleeping, false courage, poor search, bad position, apathy and pre-
occupation as some of these elements. All are related to carelessness.

Brooks's presentation stems from his earlier experience as a member
of the Los Angeles Police Department's special investigations team, the
unit called into action after any shooting of a Los Angeles officer. Com-
prised of experienced investigators, this team is responsible for reconstructing all officer-involved shootings in the city which resulted in the
injury or death of any person. The resources and numerical strength of
the Los Angeles Police Department justify the creation of such a special
after-action investigations team. This concept is feasible for all but the
smallest departments to embrace, too. These smaller departments may
make arrangements to call upon a larger force to help on an "as needed"
basis with reconstructing a case.

The importance of developing an officer survival program based on
local circumstances cannot be over-emphasized. Whenever there is a
serious or fatal attack on an officer, not only a thorough investigation,
but complete analysis is needed. Both may prove of extraordinary value
in drawing up subsequent training simulations, revising field procedures and hopefully in the prevention of future officer deaths.

By no means is Brooks's book and survival training course the only
one. There are many, many others. A book of special merit is **Street
Survival: Tactics for Armed Encounters.**[4] Its writers, seasoned police
personnel, put on an impressive, widely heralded two-day street survival
seminar at various locations nationwide. The International Association
of Chiefs of Police, the Northwestern University Traffic Institute and
the California Specialized Training Institute at Camp San Luis Obispo
prepare and conduct similar seminars, too.

Several commercial enterprises have prepared survival training
seminars on video tapes and film for showing in conjunction with departmental training in survival techniques. Such media training aids are
particularly useful to forces which, because of the expense of specialized

---

[4]Ronald J. Adams, Thomas M. McTernan and Charles Remsberg, **Street Survival: Tactics
for Armed Encounters,** Northbrook, Illinois, Calibre press, 1980.

separate survival programs or the modest numerical strength or location of the departments, are unable to send personnel away to school. Video cassettes or films are available to serve as the basis on which survival techniques can be expanded for training sessions. The value of films and cassettes that address officer field survival cannot be overstated! These should be a staple in every training center.

Handling and Transporting Prisoners

The supervision and control of prisoners in the field is a regular occurrence which should never be considered or treated as routine. The fact that such a police task is treated as routine creates an urgent problem in law enforcement. Transporting prisoners presents untold dangers to all officers involved as well as to suspects. In short, no prisoner should ever be left unsupervised until he or she is secure in the jail area.

The first thing to do after a prisoner has been taken into custody is to conduct a thorough search of his or her person and clothing. Less-than-thorough searches have resulted in death for many officers. For example, in one fatal Oklahoma incident the arresting officers made an initial search of a prisoner who, later, while being transported by auto to jail in another town, murdered the officer. In their search, officers found several rounds of pistol ammunition in the suspect's pockets. Yet, even though the suspect was searched a total of three times by three different officers, they failed to uncover a small pistol taped to the suspect's upper right arm. In fact, the suspect had made a slit in his jacket for easy access to the pistol, something that also went undetected in the searches. A few hours later, while being transported, the suspect removed the pistol and murdered the officer.

The solution to incidents like this lies in better training designed to regularize and habitualize the pretransportation search of a prisoner. In the incident described above, "ammunition" should have meant "gun" to the officers and the searches should have been pressed with intensity. Moreover, written procedures about searches, methods and procedures should be produced and made mandatory reading for all officers, both in and following the police academy. A training bulletin which covers the techniques of apprehending, searching and transporting suspects should be published and should describe the department's procedures for approaching a suspect, searching him (his vehicle or his person) and handcuffing and transporting the person. The bulletin should be painstakingly precise and detailed, spelling out the very elements needed to assure proper precautions.

Officers must give close scrutiny to items which, to most people, are harmless, normal items. Such possessions as a belt buckle, pocket comb or ball point pen could cover or themselves become a potentially dangerous weapon. The FBI and some major law enforcement agencies regularly disseminate information about the newest in covert weaponry discovered on prisoners. The belt buckle might be the handle for a knife, the cutting edge hidden by the belt. The comb could house a stiletto-type spike which springs out and locks into position when a release button is pressed at one end. The ball point pen could be the casing for a five-inch needle glued into the cap.

While the safest method of transporting prisoners is by paddy wagon, not all forces, especially those of few personnel, have such special purpose vehicles. They must use standard police cars for such purposes. When that is the case the precautionary measures outlined in training manuals and academy instruction should be utilized.

Strange, unexpected and unanticipated events occur in cars. In one instance, a deputy sheriff had handcuffed and searched a prisoner and placed him in the back seat of a patrol car. In route to jail, the suspect unlatched the back of the driver's seat and suddenly shoved it forward with his feet, pinning the deputy against the steering wheel. The deputy was beaten severely before being rescued. In another instance, officers searching a suspect's car found that sometime earlier a prisoner had placed infected hypodermic syringes in the vehicle's seat cracks to hamper searches. This is about the nadir in obstructing police!

Ideally, the hands of each prisoner should be restrained so that any attempt to assault the transporting officer would be unusually awkward, if not impossible. In addition, the transporting officer, if he or she did not conduct the first search, should routinely re-search the prisoner. Handcuffs and other restraining devices should be used according to prescribed police department standards. Moreover, metallic handcuffs should meet the voluntary national standards set out by the National Institute of Law Enforcement and Criminal Justice. In addition, police training courses and manuals should set forth the proper and improper use of such devices for officers. Never be foolish enough to think that a handcuffed prisoner is harmless! Some prisoners can slip handcuffs.

Department policy may specify the circumstances which call for handcuffs, but the final decision is up to the arresting officer. His decision should be based on the officer's perception and assessment of the situation, and his responsibility to protect himself, the public and the prisoner. A suspect may be cooperative or docile at the time of arrest, but that is no guarantee that there will not be a concerted attempt later to overpower the officer or escape if an opportunity presents itself. Many prisoners appear docile and nonviolent. However, once they are in the vehicle and are heading for their moment of truth at the jail, they may react with sudden fury. Therefore, an officer should never try to second guess the prisoner's nature and on that basis decide not to restrain him. A universal hallmark of a good officer is his ability to "talk" a suspect into handcuffs for that ride to headquarters.

An officer may be shot and killed by losing control of his own service revolver while transporting a prisoner. This can happen even if a prisoner is handcuffed, though cuffs lessen the prospect. Seasoned officers who are safety conscious routinely move their revolver to the side away from the prisoner. If the officer is driving, for example, and the prisoner is to his right (which would be the logical position), the gun should be kept on the officer's left side. Uncomfortable, perhaps, but the safety margin favors the officer who takes advantage of this practical precautionary measure. The gun is out of reach to the suspect but still accessible to the driver.

Many, many felons are transported by commercial air carriers and steps should be taken to avoid incidents which may endanger not just the officers but other passengers and the aircraft, too. Along this line, Federal Aviation Regulations (FAR) Part 121.584 (a) (3) requires that:

> If the passenger is considered to be in a maximum risk category, the passenger is under the control of at least two armed law enforcement officers and no other passengers are under the control of those two . . . officers.

Officers should identify themselves and their prisoner to airline authorities as far in advance of boarding as possible. Carriers are very helpful about granting special seating requests for such transports. But officers must realize that even though there are no federal regulations prohibiting the cuffing or shackling of prisoners, most airlines will not allow passengers to be so restrained during flight either for safety or public relations purposes. The carrier's staff will also make suitable arrangements regarding firearms.

Maximum risk is an arguable term, and ideally its interpretation should rest with the jurisdiction making the transport. While by regulations, two officers should accompany dangerous prisoners, sometimes a force, because of economic limitations, assigns but one officer. Clearly, this is hazardous: forces should not sacrifice safety in air transportation for economic reasons. There is too much at stake to take a bargain basement approach to this mission.

High-Risk Warrant Executions

The need for a well conceived, carefully planned, systematic approach to high-risk warrant executions is as urgent as is the service of warrants. Seemingly so routine, warrant service is anything but a rote maneuver. A warrant service plan should be carefully thought out and implemented in advance of each service. Adequate personnel and equipment, of course, are essential, but so is the pre-incident assessment of what may be encountered during service. Lines of fire, visibility, deciding the time when best to execute, assigning roles and assuring supervision are crucial factors as well, and should not be overlooked.

Pre-incident planning includes, but is not limited to, an analyses of: (1) who (or what) is sought; (2) how many and how well armed the suspects may be; (3) their rapsheets; (4) the nature of the structure and locale, including offensive and defensive cover possibilities; (5) fields of fire; (6) entry and exits for both officers and suspects; (7) interior layout and nature of construction; (8) lighting; (9) the neighborhood and neighbors, and whether they are likely to be friendly or hostile to police; and (10) the relevant information on utilities. Photographs of suspects, the area, the structure, etc., would be helpful to have in planning, and then executing, the warrant service, too.

Officers must be reminded that the advantage in warrant service operations is with the suspects, as they are almost surely more closely acquainted with the structure's layout, the weapons they may or may not have available, and the character of the neighborhood. Moreover, the suspects know their intentions, whereas the officers can only guess as to the resolve of the thugs to fight, flee, cave in, etc. Police officer precision and orderliness are the hallmarks of well-planned high-risk warrant executions. Recognition and implementation of these procedures will help reduce the prospect of officer and suspect bloodshed.

CHAPTER V

EQUIPMENT COUNTERMEASURES

A S TECHNOLOGY expands, more and more protective devices and garments are being devised for the safety of police officers, police cars, headquarters, jails, etc. Bulletproof vests, armored vehicles, helmets, special underwear, capture nets, electric shock weapons, chemical and other items are rapidly finding their way into the commercial marketplace. Just how effective are these devices? More importantly, how many police will actually take the trouble to wear protective clothing, even if it is available and made mandatory by the force?

Commercial interests have been quick to seize upon the street scene and introduce equipment items with overblown claims of maxi-capability and mini-cost. For years, some police forces have been easy marks for fast talking salesmen. In fact, too often experience has shown that the gear falls short of claims, is unsafe, and becomes a white elephant in the police storeroom.

Fortunately, two reputable agencies have tested and evaluated many items available for police purchase. These are the Police Weapons Center of the International Association of Chiefs of Police and the Law Enforcement Assistance Administration's Law Enforcement Standards Program, housed within the U.S. Justice Department's National Institute of Law Enforcement and Criminal Justice. These two organizations serve a very useful purpose. Their evaluation reports should be sought by any force before purchasing equipment of an allegedly protective nature.

Specialized equipment can prove effective when police face varied types of field problems. Certain items can offer protection against snipers, irate motorists who turn aggressive, fleeing criminals and in other potentially life-threatening situations. There are various types of equipment and systems discussed here. However, equipment items alone

83

should never be considered as a cure-all, and no department should rely on an equipment-only system of countermeasures. Effective, career-long training remains the best protection for the always-vulnerable police officer.

DISPATCHING, TELEPHONES AND COMPUTERS

Communications centers are life saving centers for what is (or is not) done by those employees in a communications control capacity, for those persons who take incoming calls from citizens and send officers to handle the cases have immense impact on police safety. In addition, the ever increasing application of computers and systems technology to policing relates to safety, too.

Improving Radio Dispatching

The backbone of any efficient police department is its radio communications. By this means officers are kept in constant contact with headquarters, with each other and with supervisory personnel. However, an incomplete or poorly worded radio dispatch will put an officer at a disadvantage. It may also put him in a situation which could prove perilous to his life because he lacks the necessary information on the assignment, and therefore is unaware of its possible dangers. In short, radio dispatchers work quietly behind the scenes telling cops where to go and alerting them as to what may be found when they get there.

There are two problems inherent in a poor radio dispatch. One is the failure of the dispatcher to transmit by air enough pertinent information to the field officer. This is related to the second problem, that persons taking incoming telephone calls fail to secure sufficient information from the citizen to enable the radio dispatcher to give out adequate descriptive content. Inept or lazy persons handling the phones, as well as indifferent dispatchers, may easily compromise an officer's safety.

Training programs for personnel who take incoming telephone calls, as well as for radio dispatchers, must be established and be required of all communications personnel. The dispatcher's job, although technically a desk job, is far from the usual desk job. He or she must remain calm in speaking with people who call the police, even those who are obviously under extraordinary stress and are nervous to the point of near irrationality. Once basic information on a call for service has been secured, the dispatcher must informatively, yet concisely, assign police to cover the incident, regardless of what the circumstances are. This requires a calm professionalism all the time, but especially so in relaying extremely stressful and emotional calls. How and when and how completely the information is relayed and transmitted will determine, to a large extent, the success of the field officer in carrying out the assignment.

The training of telephone and dispatching personnel should include some time in the field so that they may observe first-hand the importance of the work they perform at headquarters. They should be obliged to ride on patrol and to see officers in action in order to fully appreciate the problems which can stem from misinterpretation, misinformation or no information at all. In this way, dispatchers will better understand the scope and significance of their own position and appreciate the dangers of inadequate communication. Communications personnel must understand that there should never be any question in the patrol officer's mind as to what he is supposed to do, or where and when he is to do it. If that turns out to be the case, the dispatcher has committed the cardinal sin of under-informing or mis-informing with potentially hazardous results.

Let's examine what impact a poor communication has when it is translated to operational terms. Take, for instance, the radio call to an officer, directing him to proceed to 1334 Elm to "take a call from a woman." With only that information he will be inadequately prepared to meet the possible dangers that exist if the call is actually a domestic disturbance, with a dangerous weapon in the hands of the spouse. Actually, a "call from a woman" would normally mean that she wishes to discuss a traffic matter, report a theft or needs advice of some sort. It is assumed to be routine and as such an officer will make no special assessment as to any potential for danger. Moreover, there is little chance that another nearby unit will cover since a "call from a woman" doesn't imply danger. The whole issue of effective communications pivots on the point of police officer early-awareness. Dispatchers must never forget that an alert officer, early-warned by radio, is less susceptible to the inherent dangers of a situation than an uninformed officer.

As yet there are no sure means devised that will cause an officer to be mentally alert to all possible factors in a given situation. But there are means to insure that an officer will at least receive the most complete information available about the situation from the communications center at headquarters.

Improved dispatching procedures are important in all field operations. They are especially crucial in situations where officers are being sent to a robbery or burglary alarm, calls involving people who may be mentally unstable or have been drinking, a call reporting a felony in progress or to domestic disturbances. In any hot case, all officers involved should be advised of the nature of the report and given the relevant details, insofar as they may be known, and assigned to specific duty by the dispatcher. Vastly improved telephone answering and radio dispatching procedures and the use of a standard dispatching signal code will hopefully lead to greater officer awareness, hence safety.

There is an additional element to assuring the finest possible radio call dispatching. It is making certain that street cops fully understand the problems dispatchers face and what dispatching involves. So street cops should, as part of their training, be obliged to observe the dispatch center staff at work. Better yet, if circumstances allow, street officers should have to actually work dispatch sometime!

The dispatcher occupies a pivotal position in assuring officer safety. On the one hand, the dispatcher should remain uninvolved emotionally in the activities of officers and emergency callers, while simultaneously being concerned, perceptive, inquiring and sincere. These kinds of qualities are best fostered through extensive dispatcher training, coupled with experience and on-the-job evaluation. Yet training alone is not the only immediate solution to providing officers on patrol with quicker, more complete and detailed information about a call. For the officer's safety, there are new communication products on the market that will facilitate greater officer safety through improved communication.

Combined Communications

More and more forces are amalgamating telephone and radio communications so that one modern, sophisticated, well equipped center can serve the needs of a region. Centralized police dispatch can assure that all forces in a region, including very small ones, have around-the-clock, seven day service. It will also eliminate the overlap, confusion and duplication so often common to individual systems in a region. It can be cost efficient, too, as it maximizes the number of dispatch personnel, makes their training easier and will readily accommodate a 911 emergency telephone system for a region. The virtues of combined communications (and records keeping, too) are many and can contribute to a higher order of safety for police.

Electronic Processing Systems

Computers are being used by several large forces to decrease the time required to process calls for service. For example, in one system the dispatcher types the address of an urgent call onto a video terminal. Within moments a computer verifies the address and gives a geographical location. The distress call is beamed to the nearest patrol cars and printed out on paper by facsimile transmission for the officers to read in their patrol units. Within seven seconds, the officers acknowledge the call and are responding.

This type of procedure and equipment helps cut down the chance of an officer making an error in taking down a radio call. With less chance of error in transcribing the dispatch, there is less chance of an officer getting the wrong read on a situation and going in unprepared, or worse yet, not alert to the dangers of the call. Officer safety is enhanced due to the speed with which vehicle license plate and name checks can be transmitted from the field, processed by the minicomputer and returned.

Another computer-based police dispatching system offers immediate communicable response when an emergency call is received by the dispatcher. While most of a department's calls for assistance each day are routine, when an emergency comes in, it gets top priority. That's when no time must be wasted in recording and dispatching pertinent information needed for a prompt response.

When a call for assistance is received by police telephone, a police complaint operator asks a few key questions. Then the operator types the address of the incident into a computer-aided dispatching system. Now polled, at once the system indicates the "street to beat" response sequence in the computer. The computer links the address with the proper motor patrol area, census tract and radio frequency of assignment. This information appears on a TV screen at the console of the appropriate radio dispatch operator handling that frequency. Moreover, the TV screen shows the dispatcher which units are available for dispatch. After selecting appropriate units and assigning them, the dispatcher clears his screen and begins to handle the next highest priority call which awaits attention.

Electronic Car Locators

Electronic car locators are helpful in saving lives. An incident involving a highway patrol trooper slain on a lonely country road is illustrative. In this incident the dispatcher's office had no fix on the whereabouts of the trooper or his patrol car. All that was known was that the trooper was stopping an auto somewhere. A few frenzied hours later, thanks to a call from a passing motorist, police converged on an ugly scene. They found the trooper murdered, the patrol car's red lights still flashing.

How much earlier had the murder been committed? Who had the officer stopped? What cars were seen on the road shortly after the shooting took place? Investigators were unable to answer these questions at once because the trooper had failed to advise headquarters as to whom he was stopping and where. This is exactly the type of incident in which a car locator system would have had premium value, perhaps even life-saving!

If the department had had an electronic car locator looped into its dispatching center, the communications personnel would have known where the trooper had made the stop, even if for some reason he had been unable to radio headquarters and give the site. As it was, substantial time elapsed before the disaster came to police attention which may account for the fact that it was about seven months until a suspect was taken into custody, charged and convicted.

An electronic car locator system would enhance officer safety. It is designed so each mobile unit will have an emergency status button which will provide a continuous electronic link to a department's communications center. Moreover, officers in need of help may instantly designate their location and status without need to rely on voice communications and their alarm will be received. The digital system reduces the necessity of actual voice transmission and decreases radio channel congestion by perhaps up to 33 percent, further enhancing officer safety by freeing air time for urgent voice messages.

Whether emergency conditions or carelessness cause an officer to fail to radio his or her position, the interests of safety demand that an officer's location be pinpointed at a moment's notice. And since it is advantageous to dispatch the car nearest to a request for help, the car locator system allows for greater patrol efficiency and time saving.

Personal Portable Radio Gear

Today it is common for officers to be routinely equipped with portable personal radios. These are modern, utilitarian, specifically-designed, hand-held radio transmitting and receiving instruments. They are one of the most-important-ever innovations in police communications equipment and regularly prove their merit in enhancing safety and facilitating operations.

The advantages are noteworthy. For instance, should an officer be on assignment or investigation away from his patrol car, he is no longer out of touch with the communications center. In fact, increased safety is a hallmark of this gear. In some violent gunfire incidents in which the officer is out of touch with his patrol car's radio, a call for assistance on the portable unit could be of more lifesaving help than the officer's service revolver.

Portable radios offer other safety advantages. Perhaps an officer will see a badly wanted suspect and instead of being obliged to make a single-handed effort at capture, he may use his radio to alert all units in the area of his need for assistance. Clearly this is prudence — made possible by the significant safety increment inherent in portable radio gear. The instrument is easily affixed to the officer's uniform (the microphone/receiver may be attached to his shoulder, with the walkie-talkie portion of the unit tied to his belt), and lightweight enough so as not to cause undue discomfort or encumbrance.

Across the nation, police administrators and patrol officers are enthusiastic over this totally mobile communication system. Those who don't have it, seek it. Just why becomes apparent in a recent Oklahoma incident. Two police officers were chasing armed burglars on foot, at night, through a residential neighborhood. Far from their patrol car's radio, they were unable to summon assistance in their pursuit. Had they been equipped with today's portable radio gear, they could have radioed for help while still pursuing the criminals. As it turned out, when the officers finally cornered the two burglary suspects, the ensuing gunfight left one officer dead.

911: A National Emergency Phone Number

Although there has been steady movement nationwide to implement a national emergency police number, or the 911 system, the concept is by no means yet fully embraced. It should be, for inherent in the 911 system is immense life saving potential for everyone.

The value of having but one police emergency number across the nation is evident. It could lead to getting police to trouble calls much more quickly than before, hopefully before situations deteriorate and require extensive police intervention. Once a situation deteriorates into violence, the risk to the safety and well-being of everyone increases. Moreover, the standardized national emergency number could reduce response time to non-violent crimes, too, and enhance the prospect of arresting suspects on the job, thus removing criminals who might, at a later date, resort to violent means, like firing at police, in order to successfully complete their illegal acts.

Another advantage is to facilitate direct communication between the calling party and the police dispatcher and to reduce the time it takes police to respond to emergencies. Most citizens can remember a three-digit, nationally-used emergency number and would call that number directly instead of the operator for emergencies. Police headquarters would then be able to obtain from the caller any additional facts the officer on patrol would need to know for safety, and not depend on the memory of the telephone operator.

Technology is such that a conventional 911 system can be upgraded so that communications technicians at the 911 center are aware of a caller's address and phone number without asking a single question. So enhanced, it could also be programmed to include the name of the resident or business, type of phone—residence, business, coin—and the nearest police, fire or ambulance unit. These remarkable life saving possibilities are inherent in the "Enhanced 911" system, called E-911 in those places that have opted for these features.

There are some issues which must be resolved when a community contemplates the implementation of a 911 or an E-911 telephone system. One is who will pay for it and by what formula. Also, to what extent, if any, will state and/or federal funds be made available? A popular means of allocating costs, when the system is to serve a region, is to bill agencies on a head-count (population) basis among participating communities.

After cost issues have been resolved, there is an urgent need to educate the public as to how the system works, what it is for and of the call screening criteria. Concurrently, communications personnel must be trained in the system, its goals, mechanics, etc. In addition, each department must assure that it has sufficient backup communications systems and an emergency power source supplement so that communications may be maintained instantly during power outages.

Computerized Information Systems

There has been a need for a system that could help police to early identify hostility stemming from traffic stops and other police-citizen contacts. This need has resulted in the development of several computer based information systems patterned after the FBI's National Crime Information Center (NCIC). The FBI system is a computerized method of obtaining information on badly wanted felons, stolen cars, hot guns, and so forth. It is a nationwide system with a high threshold of entry and therefore does not include information on local crimes and wants.

There is a need for computer based information systems of yet a lower threshold of inquiry which are geared to strictly local information and wants. Such systems have been designed as backup for the NCIC and are operational in several places. For example, the greater Kansas City area is served by a highly advanced computer-based police information system called ALERT, an acronym for the Automated Law Enforcement Response Team. The Kansas City network was designed to keep local records of stolen vehicles, wanted persons, aliases used by criminals, current lists of fugitives, and crime reporting statistics and make this information readily available to police upon local inquiry. The Kansas City system has been coordinated with the FBI's NCIC in Washington, D.C.

Several other types of locally-based systems can be designed to supplement the NCIC and ALERT type networks. These can include an automated firearm system, an automated property system, a stolen vehicle system, a wanted persons system, a criminal history system, a police information network, etc.

When there are automated information systems there must be training about how and under what conditions officers are to access the data banks. Officers must be trained to be computer-literate and proficient in polling those which are available to aid them in the performance of their duties. As more and more computers are used in law enforcement, the listing of all the various systems, as well as their purpose and availability, is indispensable.

BODY PROTECTIVE EQUIPMENT

The concept of protecting one's body by virtue of a shield or specially designed apparel is as old as war itself. Police have need for such armor because of the nature of their role. Spurred by the massive disorders of the 60s and 70s and by the dramatic increase in officer murders, the protective equipment industry has been on a research, development and marketing binge. Some of the products have helped protect officers.

Bulletproof Vests and Jackets

A majority of all officers murdered on duty are victims of gunshots which hit them in the upper chest or upper back. These victims, for the most part, received wounds in areas which would have been protected by ballistic vests had the victims been wearing them. Ironically, some of the victims were wearing vests but they took hits in areas not covered by the garments, as in the underarm area, the neck line or the lower abdomen. Notwithstanding these exceptions, bulletproof vests and jackets have become life savers in a big way—and if more officers would wear them there would be still fewer casualties.

A few years ago, a motorcycle officer on an impulse purchased a bulletproof vest. The investment was to save his life, as shortly after the purchase he was shot by a motorist to whom he was issuing a ticket. Injuries? The officer suffered only a bruise. Two weeks later, another officer was only slightly injured when a motorist fired a bullet at his heart. He was also wearing a bulletproof vest. Soon after the incident, the city council ordered that bulletproof vests become standard equipment for the city's 7,000 police. At a cost of around $50 a vest, the city expended $350,000. This purchase proved to be highly cost-effective in terms of officer safety and morale, time on the job saved from injury-related absence and medical and pension benefit expenditures.

For years, departments across the nation have been seeking a lightweight, undetectable, yet comfortable, bulletproof vest. In 1974 the Law Enforcement Assistance Administration started overseeing the preparation of lightweight and inconspicuous protective garments for law enforcement. The garments use a synthetic fabric called kevlar which can be integrated into current police uniforms or work as a separate vest. The LEAA contracted with the Aerospace Corporation of El Segundo, California to fabricate the vests and run a series of ballistic and other related tests.

Tests conducted on the kevlar fabric concluded that it was a highly efficient protective material. When fashioned into a jacket or vest-type garment, it has been shown to protect against approximately 30 percent of guns of all types tested, and was even more effective against blunt shots fired from 90 to 95 percent of all United States handguns. But the stumbling block appears to be persuading officers to wear the garments. Although current models weigh but a few pounds, the vests are reported to cause discomfort when worn during the hot summer months. Yet it is during these months that studies show many officers are attacked.

The material's effectiveness seems proven. In fact there are now no known corporations manufacturing soft body armor that do not meet standards set out by the Law Enforcement Safety Laboratory of the U.S. Bureau of Standards.

The decision of whether or not to employ bulletproof vests, of course, rests with each department. However, every police and sheriff's department should be familiar with the availability of these devices and should evaluate their safety within the context of local conditions.

Police officers are beginning to see suspects wearing kevlar vests. For example, the Elmira, New York police found themselves in a shootout with kidnapping suspects in January, 1984. One suspect was killed by police fire while the second committed suicide. Both were heavily armed and wearing protective vests. As with the officers previously discussed who were injured while wearing protective garments, one of these suspects sustained a fatal wound in other than the protected areas.

If a force requires its personnel to wear protective garments, preparations must be taken to ease a resultant problem. This is the prospect that the garments may produce loss of body salt and excessive perspiration especially during hot weather. Officers, alert to the problem, should consider supplementing their salt intake with tablets. The department may advise officers of the necessity to take seasonal precautionary measures prescribed by the public health physician.

Riot Helmets and Other Body Armor

The Law Enforcement Standards Program was created as a result of the Omnibus Crime Control and Safe Streets Act of 1968 and was designed to develop and test new and improved techniques, systems and equipment. Its standard for a police riot helmet declared: ". . . they [the helmets] are not generally designed to offer protection against gunfire." The need for such a helmet is readily apparent on certain types of assignments such as flushing out gunmen, at hostage-taking incidents and during barricades and roadblocks. They may be helpful during certain types of raids, too.

Helmets, though, tend to be uncomfortable when worn for long periods and may restrict an officer's movement. But where a specific type of incident is anticipated and could be potentially dangerous, the wearing of helmets for that mission makes sense.

Helmets must be designed to protect against blows to the side of the head as well as those to the top. A utilitarian helmet is not going to resemble the normal police software cap. Rather, it will be similar to a motorcycle helmet design. The visor must also have good impact strength, while being made of a clear plastic, lightweight material. Of course, there must be adequate ventilation, along with a form of stripping which will prevent liquids from running down the helmet and onto the officer's face.

Research is also underway into the area of bulletproof face shields, bulletproof groin and leg protectors, and even full body armor and shields. The practicality of officers routinely wearing such apparel poses drawbacks to the feasibility and effectiveness of assorted bulletproof and other protective masks, clothing and shields. However, when seeking an unlocated sniper or waiting out a hostage and barricaded criminal situation, wearing body armor or taking cover behind a shield makes sense. But for routine patrol duties in cities in the hot south central United States during the summer months, for example, body armor may not be so appealing.

De-Militarizing Police Officer Appearance

Rather than adopting defensive wearing apparel in hopes of saving police lives, at one time some forces put their street cops in sport coats or blazers to soothe potentially dangerous police-citizen encounters. No longer wearing the traditional dark uniforms, officers so clad hardly looked like typical men-in-blue. These forces sought to eliminate one image of the "traditional" police by projecting a sense of police "service" rather than police "force."

In terms of protective clothing, the blazers hardly offered the protection of a bulletproof vest. Rather, they were intended as a means of blunting the outright hostility that the traditional uniform is said to incite in some citizens. So the blazers were intended to bring about safety by other means. Whether the jackets have had such an effect is unknown, but the concept underscores the belief that how an officer appears may defuse what could otherwise by a violent confrontation between police and citizens. The theory, in essence, is that clothes make the (man or woman) officer! But does it really work?

In a similar but less dramatic move in the late sixties, many police departments had officers wear a shoulder patch replica of the American flag on their uniforms. Some forces put a flag decal on police vehicles, too. The trend began in the wake of disrespect shown the colors by draft protestors, campus agitators and flag-burners. Some police officials credited the measure with preventing assaults on officers. While hard to document, the measure showed that police administrators perceived a need to counteract outward displays of hostility and aggression.

Wearing flag symbols or sport-coat-like blazers were both responses on the part of police departments which had became urgently aware of violent, anti-police aggression. These were measures selected to counteract the violence. The changes in apparel characterize police sincerity in serving the public without compromising officer safety. However, the ideas themselves are not the complete solution. What is needed is more analysis by competent scholar-researchers of the timeworn problem of cop fighting.

SPECIAL DETECTION DEVICES

Harsh as it may sound, incidents do occur in which the only safe course of action available to police is justifiable homicide. Take, for example, an instance where a mentally deranged person has positioned himself strategically and is firing randomly on citizens. It may be that the only realistic solution is to kill the suspect which is unfortunate. What is more unfortunate is that the sophisticated weaponry and detection devices that in many instances could help officers safely handle such an incident are not widely available in many police forces today.

In some sniper attacks the police have tried to flush out the gunman by using canine units or special weapons teams. In some incidents officers have been murdered while trying to stop the sniper. One of the problems may be that the police cannot pinpoint the location of the sniper. Searching devices are needed that have the capacity to uncover a sniper very soon after he has taken overt action. Technology has developed such devices in the weaponry and equipment of the armed forces. It's application to law enforcement is obvious, and it should be made available to police, too.

In particular, the development of a night vision device should be encouraged to permit police to probe into hallways, dark alleys, fields and streets without sacrificing their own protective cover. The device should be lightweight and inexpensive to permit its use on regular patrol. It would surely make night patrol work, store security, checking and searches safer for police. Hopefully, the same devices, if keyed to sense body heat or some other physical characteristic to disclose a person from far away, could be applied to daytime situations, as well.

High-powered rifles, with extensive fine sighting equipment, are essential to have on that occasion when a suspect has isolated himself and has taken the lives of others. If an individual department lacks the money for weaponry, specific prior arrangements should be made to borrow the gear from the state or a nearby local force or from a military facility in the vicinity. Ideally, the nearby forces would provide not only the weapons, but the personnel skilled in their use.

Law enforcement agencies urgently need sophisticated search-and-destroy equipment. Without it, police administrators risk a regrettable incident: the murders of their own officers as well as, possibly, of unsuspecting citizens.

CHAPTER VI

TWO SPECIAL ENTERPRISES:
JAILING AND UNDERCOVER ROLES

UNDERCOVER WORK has always been hazardous and recognized as such. Jailing is also a hazardous role but has never been adequately so identified. Steps, set out in this chapter, can be taken to minimize the danger of serving in these roles.

JAIL COUNTERMEASURES

Keeping a suspect within a confined area, such as in an automobile or the security section of a jail or prison, is far more hazardous than most people would ever imagine. This is because suspects are supposedly subdued and under control by the time they reach the jail or prison. Seemingly contrite prisoners can burst into a sudden physical frenzy, catching the staff off guard. Attacks on officers which occur in supposedly secure areas should be of major concern to police administrators. In a sense, custody is a game of chess between prisoners and officers.

Why would an already secure area be so dangerous? It is partly because jailers across the nation may be victimized by handmade weapons, some crude, others ingenious, but both very deadly. An even more dangerous factor is the ruthlessness on the part of inmates who seek to escape. Taken together, the two factors work an ever-present danger to corrections and custody personnel in state prisons and county jails, as well as city lockups.

Remarkably, none of the 54 Oklahoma police victims studied was killed as a result of a jail or prison breakout. But five persons who had escaped from prison or jail, and six others being transported there, combined to murder 12 of the 54 officers slain in Oklahoma over the 35 years 1950-1984. Clearly, police have a stake in the safety and security aspects of detention facilities.

That no police were killed during a jail or prison breakout does not indicate that prison breaks are outdated, or that the county jails and city lockups in Oklahoma are so secure that escape is impossible. On the contrary; rural jails, not only in Oklahoma but throughout the United States, are extremely vulnerable to escape. So are some city lockups. One long-range solution lies in the appropriation of more funds to corrections. But for short-range solutions, extra precautionary methods need to be taken by corrections personnel at all three levels of government: state, county and local.

The Hazard Inherent in Jails and Lockups

County jails and city lockups are at least as hazardous to the police who staff them as are state prisons to guards for a number of reasons. Two of these are poor physical facilities and overcrowding.

In spite of jail standards, many of the facilities are old, not well maintained and were not well designed initially. Some are so old that cell doors, including those housing felony suspects, are secured only by chains and padlocks. Some jails across America have inadequate medical facilities, if any at all, and several have inadequate toilet facilities. Finally, many jails have neither exercise nor recreation facilities and are so crowded that the staff is unable to segregate classes of prisoners.

In 1981, the Advisory Commission on Intergovernmental Relations reported that there were 3,343 county jails and 13,566 local holding and pre-trial detention facilities across America. In fact, of the 3,343 jails, 888 predate 1925 while 768 were opened from 1925 to 1950.

The Bureau of Justice Statistics reports that in 1983, 209,582 persons were held in jails and lockups out of the approximately 7 million admissions that year. Moreover, there were 70,517 staff employed in these 16,909 facilities. About one out of every eight jails had some type of in-house medical facility, although in relative terms such facilities were commonplace only in large institutions. Slightly more than three of every five jails provided their inmates with some form of recreational facilities or entertainment. Such diversion was highly limited except in large institutions, and was totally lacking in many small and medium sized jails.

Overcrowding joins obsolescence as pernicious problems nationwide. Too many people in too small an area, especially when facilities are old and deteriorating, adds up to a dangerous situation for inmates and staff alike, especially when the prisoners are convicted or suspected criminals, capable of aggressive acts. Although many state prisons are overcrowded too, and some are very old, the problem seems of greater magnitude on the local level. The conditions are exacerbated because many felons are held in county jails because state prisons are beyond capacity. This makes jails even more dangerous.

There are three factors in county and city jails which are alarming. First, some jail personnel are part-time untrained employees. Second, not all full-time jail employees have received sufficient training in jailing, security procedures, searching, and so forth. Third, many street cops know the jail only insofar as booking is involved. Clearly, there is a need for professionals to serve in jailing roles.

Jailing, in contrast to patrol, is a fixed position post which must be staffed on a regular basis with field personnel assigned on short notice. Most street officers are neither trained in jailing nor motivated for their short-term roles. Duty in the jail is seen by street cops as an unpopular assignment, a virtual eight hours in Siberia. It is a stigma post. Several of the officers victimized in the jail were street personnel who, on a moment's notice, were assigned to serve a duty tour as a jailor. They filled in for a regular jailor who, for some reason, was off duty.

Other officers victimized in jail were patrol or detective personnel who, while booking their prisoners, were caught by a sudden attack. The booking desk is a highly likely site for violence in the jail, as is the elevator leading to the jail.

Guns in jail are an invitation to mayhem. Dismayingly, in some forces officers are allowed to routinely wear their firearms while in the jail security sector. Moreover, in some jails, field personnel are allowed to wear their firearms when in the process of booking prisoners. These practices are an invitation to gun-grabbing and shooting incidents. Unsecured firearms in jail facilities violate every principle of accepted jail management and police procedure. It is an inexcusably careless act.

In some places, both the age and location of the jail within the headquarters structure contributed to assaults on officers. For example, one city had its jail located so that the female detention area was visible to anyone coming into headquarters! When male prisoners were brought into the station for booking, an inordinate number of assaults took place as the men were taken past the area where the females looked out. In all probability, male suspects were showing off for females in custody, attacking officers to attract attention to their macho!

Police administrators should have a prime concern in making jail facilities secure in order to reduce escape risk and disorder. But most jail security problems seem linked to personnel failure or lack of training, not physical design. Therefore it is essential that personnel assigned to jail roles should receive thorough training and regular re-training in security principles. This training should also apply to all personnel, including commanders, subject to short-term, time-limited assignments as relief in jails.

County jails and city lockups appear to suffer from another problem: overlapping administration. This problem stems from the fact that county commissioners must fund the jail while the sheriff has control over its administration and the admission and release of the daily population, but not its funding. The result is overcrowding, assaults on jailers and other prisoners, and a breakdown in overall jail security. These three elements have been the fertile breeding ground for hostage taking situations and have resulted in some fatal attacks on jailers by prisoners. Occasionally, visitors get caught in the middle of these capers.

Many counties and cities have failed to commit adequate funds for upgrading county jails and city lockups. Yet the social and political pressures on sheriffs and police chiefs to up-grade, reconstruct, and expand prisoner facilities has intensified. Demands are made to provide rehabilitation programs and services for convicted prisoners. Periodic state and federal inspections, and sometimes local grand jury reports, force the issues. So does the adoption of jail standards.

The solution lies in embracing measure intended to reduce county jail admissions and to speed up releases. County boards of commissioners should talk earnestly with the police and judges to develop plans for safer facilities and improved programs. Among the problems are postponements for both pre-sentence investigations and delays by judges in getting out orders for moving convicted prisoners to the state penitentiary after sentencing. The police and judges need a plan to relieve the county jail and city lockups of unnecessary operational expense. Enhanced safety needs must be met, too.

It is also timely for cities and counties which are facing the need to build a new jail to confer with one another on whether joint facilities arrangements could be worked out, with one jail serving an urbanized area. Resource pooling of this sort seems to make fiscal sense, appears efficient in handling prisoners, capitalizes on economies of scale, and enhances recruitment, training and retention of professional custodial staff. Moreover, jail consolidation has been consistently encouraged by respected government study groups, and in most places where a regional jail has been opened, it is working successfully.

Jail consolidation is neither new nor unusual. Cleveland County, Oklahoma, handles all of the prisoners for the City of Norman; Goodhue County and Red Wing, Minnesota, have merged jails, as have the forces of the City and County of Denver, Colorado. Moreover, Berkeley, California, has housed prisoners from the neighboring City of Albany for over 40 years. Some other prominent examples where cities have merged their jails with counties are found in the City of Phoenix and Maricopa County, Arizona; the City of Miami and Dade County, Florida; and Tucson and Pima County, Arizona. Amalgamation of jails may not solve every problem, but the move should help improve security, prove cost efficient and reduce attacks on jailers in the nation's city and county institutions.

Some state corrections systems have assembled a special unit which goes on line as soon as an escape has been detected. This is a team of investigators which will work full-time to track down the escapee. They begin by talking with persons who have visited or phoned the inmate most often and most recently. Contacts will also be made with those who have written the prisoner, as well as with his family and friends. This suggests that an impressive array of intelligence is often crucial to recapturing suspects before they have a chance to get into extensive additional trouble. Very large county jails may form similar units for activation when an escape has been detected.

Searching for Contraband

Jail personnel in every jail or lockup should conduct periodic, but not pre-scheduled, comprehensive searches for contraband. Vehicles in which prisoners ride, rooms in which they are questioned and cells where they await court appearances should be shaken down often, on unannounced occasions. Items uncovered are usually routine, but can spell trouble. Such things as pencils, combs and mess hall utensils might, when sharpened, become weapons. A paper clip or a ball point pen cartridge may be fashioned to pick handcuff locks. Occasionally innovative contraband turns up, illustrating the inventiveness and determination born of desperation among people in custody. A full array of dangerous weapons, some crudely fashioned, others beautifully tooled, may be uncovered. Cell searches are important for the safety not just of jail personnel but for other inmates as well as visitors, too.

Some jails and prisons have formed specialized security squads to fight the increasing problem of contraband items. These units ferret out thousands of dangerous weapons each year. These squads are essential since ordinary security measures rarely cope with the ingenuity inmates show in handcrafting weapons. In addition to weapons, the squad sometimes discovers escape-kits which include grapples, ropes, saws, and so forth, and illegal pills, narcotics and money. Specialized security squad members may play another role by giving inservice training classes for corrections personnel and recommending and reporting on security strength of prisons.

A similar security squad could be formed to operate on a local or regional basis to analyze and inspect county jails and city lockups. The squad could also train local corrections and police personnel. As a practical matter, if a state opted to provide this service, the team could be based at the state penitentiary and be funded as part of the corrections budget. This concept is but one of many countermeasures available to making jails and lockups safer places for staff and inmates.

Corrections Alert Systems

Guards at penal facilities across the country are highly susceptible to attacks by vicious and disgruntled inmates. A technological system has been designed and implemented in one major prison to make work performance and the work environment safer. It may be adapted for implementation in county jails, too.

The system works like this. At the prison a communications/security system helps guards to enhance the safety atmosphere of the facility without sacrificing security. The system consists of having preset numerical telephone dialing combinations by which prison staff may indicate the state of security in a certain area. A communications/security center monitors the guard outposts and other areas of the prison by a series of coded lights from telephones in different areas. Guards dial a precoded number to report the security status at their stations. For example, a dark lamp on the light panel will represent an idle telephone; a white lamp indicates a busy phone. An amber light means an officer is reporting; a red lamp indicates a fire report. A green lamp indicates a telephone removed without dialing within the specified time required, or that trouble exists on the line. Amber and red flashing together mean the line has been cut or has been tampered with. The prison guards merely report in by dialing a specified code number suited to existing security conditions which, in turn, lights up the central control monitor.

The system also features a line load control, eliminating the possibility of jamming the telephone network by a coordinated effort from prisoners. A continuous line test is in effect for each station and will report on any unusual condition, such as a telephone being torn loose. The comprehensiveness of such a communications/security system allows personnel to put greater emphasis on correctional, rather than punitive, work. Ideally, an offshoot of this type of technology in prisons may be an increase in rehabilitation. If that occurs, then perhaps attacks on police by convicts will decrease.

Pretrial Diversion Programs

As shown in Part I, it is not unusual for suspects in the murder of a police officer to have been arrested prior to the fatal incident. Yet by no means was an arrest always followed by a conviction in these earlier cases. Insufficient evidence, the nature of the crime, prosecutor's discretion, plea bargaining and so forth, result in some cases falling out of the judicial system at various points short of conviction.

There exists, then, a need for viable alternatives to conviction and incarceration of persons suspected of not-so-important crimes of nonviolent nature. This is because prison, as many people in a host of professional roles readily concede, is but a breeding ground for more crime. Incarceration is the usual form of disposition, but not necessarily the best.

A possible avenue, then, would be to enact legislation which would enable the court to sentence nonviolent criminals to institutions unlike a prison environment, but rather featuring an atmosphere of rehabilitation. One form of disposition, the pretrial diversion, is an alternative to either prosecuting or dismissing charges. This program, used on state and local levels for many years, has now been introduced at the federal level. In such a program law-breakers are offered a chance to avoid trial and the stigma of a criminal record if they satisfactorily complete an individually-tailored preplanned rehabilitation program. Thus, federal attorneys, the equivalent of a state's district or prosecuting attorney, grant to certain offenders they feel are not likely to become repeat offenders, the opportunity to take part in a closely-supervised, community-based rehabilitation program. The individual, upon advice of counsel, signs a contract with the United States attorney agreeing to take part in the voluntary program for a fixed period of up to a year. The offender waives the right to a speedy trial and the statute of limitations on the offense. Participation in the program is not an admission of guilt, nor are records admissible in court.

The advantages of a program such as this in preventing future murders of police are long-range. If nonviolent offenders are steered into a pretrial diversion program and live up to the terms, the chance of committing crimes in the future is lessened. On the other hand, if these suspects go to trial, are convicted and sent to a prison, the chance that they will be rehabilitated is minimal because of the nature of the prison environment. Pretrial diversion, then, offers a two-fold advantage to police officers. First, it may well adjudicate offenders who might otherwise make it back to the streets by beating charges. Second, diversion might serve to redirect, rather than reinforce, criminal behavior. Either way the police officer stands to be safer.

UNDERCOVER LAW ENFORCEMENT

As the number, type and nature of police undercover operations grows, officers are encountering a host of new hazards. This is especially so in the narcotics law enforcement world which is increasingly characterized by the no-holds-barred nature of resistance by thugs.

There is nothing clean, sportsmanlike or honorable about the undercover and narcotics scene, anywhere. It is a world of sleazy people dealing for high stakes in the face of incredibly heavy penal sanctions should they be caught and convicted. Dopers are violent and gunfire is increasingly a part of drug arrests. Moreover, police drug investigations are involving more and more people from South America where violence is a way of life. Small wonder crooks at all levels in the business shoot first and ask questions later for they have little to lose.

What this means to police in undercover narcotics roles is that the uncertainties accompanying such work are immense even though almost every enforcement effort features several officers, in differing roles, working closely together. Although some of the finest of communications technology is used by police and in spite of concerted efforts to make undercover police operations safer, there are invariably casualties.

Greater attention must be given to assuring officer safety in undercover roles.

As in other types of police-citizen transactions, carelessness continues to plague undercover cops. For example, there are still officers wounded and killed while serving search or arrest warrants when shots are fired blindly through doors by suspects inside the premises where entry is sought. Officers, irrespective of role or assignment, should never stand in front of doorways.

It is almost standard procedure to put body transmitters with their own power sources on undercover officers who are dealing with narcotics or vice suspects. There are many hazards in doing so but on balance the transmitters are more likely to contribute to rather than detract from an officer's safety. However, in planning undercover operations which include body transmitters, contingency plans must be made for a prompt response and a rescue operation should the transmitter be discovered on the officer. The plan, of course, is going to depend on having cover personnel nearby and may also include a diversionary act. Whatever the rescue scheme, all hands must be briefed on it in advance of the operation and must instantly recognize when it has to be implemented. That is when roles change and pre-planned schemes must go into operation.

Misidentity of Officers by Other Officers

Armed confrontations by police with other officers are a growing problem with the upsurge in undercover operations, raids and warrant executions. Spelling out just how officers can be made known to other police during covert operations is a special, but urgent, problem. This applies particularly to officers who are working deeply undercover in plainclothes roles. Female officers are no exception. Clearly, these personnel run a special risk of being mistaken for thugs while performing their dangerous covert duties.

At issue is whether or not a plainclothes officer on a deeply covert operation can perform his mission with anonymity in the eyes of the public and yet be readily identifiable as an officer to other police. Realistically, the answer is negative. Yet hundreds of officers face the harrowing prospect that they suddenly find themselves in a life-threatening situation with other officers who do not realize all the actors are on the same side! It's a stressful prospect.

There is no simple standard means by which an undercover officer may, with certainty and at once, identify himself or herself as police short of blowing all that has gone into the operation earlier. In addition, not many forces have tried to implement a set procedure for making such an identification, and those that have have not found the scheme to work with certainty. The result is that those forces which have recognized the need to devise a scheme to prevent the misidentification of officers have implemented the procedure only for particular cases. These include, for example, special procedures to be in effect during raids, narcotics deals in which covert officers must be covered, during presidential visits, etc.

The most common schemes have plainclothes personnel wearing or displaying some unique, but unobtrusive, pin, badge, garment, sweat band, cap, etc. Sometimes a specific verbal command or password is given, with a precise predetermined response as conditions warrant. The utility of such schemes is speculative but some procedure is better than none, given the nature of the problem and the grave hazards undercover officers face from being accidentally victimized by other officers.

The St. Louis County police issue "raid jackets" to personnel who are in civilian clothes but who are going to serve on raiding squads. The uniquely colored jackets, when worn, are intended to enable all police personnel, whether in plainclothes or uniform, to be able to distinguish between lawmen and criminals during undercover raid situations.

A cardinal rule with regard to officer safety in covert circumstances is that the burden of initiating identification must always rest with the officer being challenged. This person must quickly convey his identity to uniformed personnel as best he or she can, perhaps even unconventionally if need calls for it. Hopefully, however, the means of conveying one's true role should be by following the identification procedures agreed to and set out in the pre-incident briefing of all hands.

Counter-Surveillance

Sometimes police find themselves targets of counter-surveillance personnel working as part of sophisticated gangs whose mission is drugs, gambling, burglary, etc. Such measures by big league criminal gangs make police work even more dangerous, raising the stress level of law enforcement personnel. While counter-surveillance is most commonly associated with big bucks drug operators, gangs doing other rip-offs have gotten into it, too.

A variety of weapons and gadgetry is used by those engaged in counter-surveillance. Electronics gear of all sorts is foremost among the hardware. An array of vehicles, including vans, are also likely to be used as are aircraft and boats, depending upon the nature of the counter-surveillance, the location of the transactions and so forth. Trained vicious dogs may also be part of a gang's counter-surveillance equipment.

What police need to be absolutely certain of is that personnel who work undercover, and those whose mission it is to cover the covert personnel, are fully trained in the pale realities of this aspect of law enforcement and how to detect signs that criminals are engaging in counter-surveillance. Also underscored is the need to assemble as much intelligence as possible about the persons with whom the police are dealing, using such intelligence to predict how the suspects may react to given circumstances. It is also crucial to carefully plan warrant services and arrests, as well as to anticipate and plan for the most likely eventualities which could spin off from a plan. In short, realize that undercover work is by no means just another day at the office: it features contacts, often one-on-one, with people who are vicious, conniving, skeptical and engaged in deals where the consequences can be suddenly fatal if the deal goes sour.

When signs of counter-surveillance are detected, police must at once anticipate that seasoned, big league, brutal crooks are at work. It is time to take a step backward and assess what is known of the suspects and to determine what, if any, additional personnel, equipment and intelligence should be brought to bear on the case. Counter-surveillance activities are the early warning signs that police may be in trouble.

Dealing with Cults and Urban Guerrillas

There seem to be more cults than ever before in American society. In fact, nationwide a host of groups whose membership believe in violence and elitist status separate from the mainstream of society have crossed swords with lawmen with disturbing frequency. The groups feature an anti-police mentality and are quick to resort to gunfire to preserve what they perceive are their First Amendment rights. Such groups have ranged from the MOVE group in Philadelphia where 80 some houses were incinerated when the police moved in in May, 1985, to a psuedo-religious cult in Memphis which took two officers hostage and tortured one, fatally injuring him.

Cults like these are anti-social, far outside the mainstream of American life. Whether organized and motivated by political, sexual, religious or environmental beliefs, cults must be of concern to police since the time will come when lawmen will be expected to deal with them in some way. Accordingly, police must endeavor to secure intelligence about the groups, their membership, mission, philosophy, armaments, etc. In addition, the dynamics of cultic organizations should be identified, analyzed and evaluated with regard to the planning of subsequent contacts and strategies. Police should realize they may be targeted by the cultists merely because officers represent the establishment and order. By appreciating these elements of cultism officers may enhance the prospects of their own survival.

Should confrontation be in the offing, there is an urgent need to anticipate the long- and short-range political and media implications which may accompany a contact. Of course, the need to anticipate the prospects of violence and property damage is paramount, too. Planning, then, and the intelligence aspects of any contact with the cults assumes gargantuan proportion. Handle with care—but with a plan—should be the hallmark of these operations. Hopefully there will be few, if any, casualties among either cops or cultists.

Urban guerrillas and terrorists are not unlike the cultists. These are persons—and groups—who for reasons of revolution, community disruption, political extremism and hatred of American institutions, use violence of all sorts to create panic. Arson, firebombing, explosive devices and ambushes or snipings are only some of the means used by terrorists to rip at society. These people reject our law, our institutions and democratic principles as they seek to intimidate people for whatever purpose motivates them.

These people and groups are a clear danger to police as well as to society as a whole. As when dealing with cultists, there must be a coordinated intelligence effort to identify and head off terrorists. There must be planning and widespread solicitations for public cooperation in dealing with these people and a firm resolve to not tolerate their bitter and diabolic violence.

O'er Amber Waves of Pot

Each year from August to October the "fall follies" take place in some parts of the United States. This is the time when police from many forces fall upon those places where illicit cash crops of marijuana are cultivated by growers for huge profits. In fact, in some locales the pot harvest is so big it's seen as the mainstay of the local economy! Lawlessness is often a partner when an illicit enterprise like pot growing assumes such significant stature. This means there is danger for police and others who seek to disrupt the undertaking.

It didn't take long for American police to begin identifying and raiding major pot fields as soon as it became public knowledge that pot growing had blossomed into a multibillion dollar business. And it didn't take long for the pot growers to cop fight in defending their fields. In fact, homemade booby traps featuring explosives and shotgun shells lodged in steel or iron devices with trip wires were found in one Oklahoma field, as were fishhooks hung head or chest high in overgrown cutting areas. Another pot grower had imbedded punji spikes in his fields while yet another had cut the rattles off of rattlesnakes and strapped the deadly reptiles to marijuana plants. Add the prospect of ambush attacks on lawmen to the litany of wounding and maiming which confronts the pot crop raiders. Such has been another day on the pot farm in the fight against pot crops. It's dangerous out there!

Pot crop raids by police have come to resemble a virtual military operation because of the violence into which lawmen may walk. This often includes overhead aerial surveillance by police helicopter crews and fixed wing aircraft—and ground shots intended to down the aircraft. Trained police dogs can help lessen the odds of violence, too, by being at the head of a field takeover and being directed to seek out snipers, booby traps and other mechanisms intended to weaken officer resolve.

On a larger front in the pot fight, prosecutors are often charging landowners and growers with tax law violations rather than pursuing violations of the relatively lax laws for cultivating marijuana. In addition, prosecutors are pushing for asset forfeiture, an angle which allows government to seize cars, equipment and real estate if such assets were acquired with the proceeds of illegal cultivation. These kinds of pressures must continue to be brought to bear on pot farmers.

Vans, Recreational Vehicles and Motor Homes

Vans, recreational vehicles and motor homes are back on America's streets and highways after several nominal sales years owing principally to surging gasoline prices. While at one time most of these vehicles were owned by 45-60 year-old couples, this is no longer so. The younger professional people with kids are surging into van and RV ownership rather than going in for luxury cars. In fact, thousands of customized vans, RVs and motor homes with extraordinary furnishings and electronic paraphernalia are on the road serving a host of purposes. Many are being used by drug dealers.

What does this mean to police? Greater danger in traffic stops because there are few tactical problems in law enforcement where officers face more unknown factors. Yet police must balance the need to protect themselves while making traffic stops with the need to treat traffic violators, almost all of whom are respectable persons, tactfully. Where vans, etc., are concerned it is a tough assignment.

It is inherently dangerous for an officer to approach a van, RV or motor home, irrespective of whether the vehicle and its occupants were pulled over for a routine stop or for a felony investigation. The design of these vehicles limits the officer's opportunity to see the occupants, inside layout, and to detect movement within. The problem is worsened immeasurably if the vehicle has darkly tinted solar glass, as many do. That there are so many possible exits from some of the vehicles exacerbates the situation as does the number of windows, the possibility of sun roofs and pop up tops, trap doors and pop out windows. There are also unlimited opportunities within vans, RVs and motor homes for persons to conceal themselves, thus able to mount a sudden, unexpected attack on an officer. Understandably, these types of vehicles are a nightmare for police in terms of officer safety.

Occupant control is crucial to officer safety during any vehicle stop. The problem with many vans, RVs and motor homes is that officers may not be readily able to see the occupants, much less be certain of how many persons are in the conveyance, and where and what they are doing. Actually being able to see a vehicle's occupants and their hands is the ideal circumstance. Hence, officers lose a substantial opportunity for control when they take on vans, RVs or motor homes. It is a disconcerting prospect.

The first tactical move in dealing with vans, RVs or motor homes is to carefully and deliberately select the spot for the stop. It should be a locale which favors the police, insofar as one may be available. Then the patrol car must be properly positioned. Next, officers must be extraordinarily alert when approaching any of these three types of vehicles, fully appreciating their tactical disadvantages from the outset. In order to even the odds, officers may begin by not drawing the police units as close to the suspect vehicle as would be done in hailing standard passenger vehicles. The additional car length affords an officer a little time during an approach, a somewhat greater chance to observe the vehicle and time to react and retreat to the squad car, if necessary. There is no rush to draw close to the suspect vehicle, hence entering the close range kill zone.

A host of general car stop/approach tactics may be in order. After radioing headquarters with the standard information about the location and purpose of the stop, description and license of the vehicle and occupants, the officer may opt to walk behind the squad car and approach the suspect vehicle from the right side. If the lawman is alone, the squad's passenger door may even be opened and slammed to simulate the presence of a second officer. During the approach the officer may be able to take advantage of a sneak peek into the cab by using the vehicle's side-mounted rear view mirrors.

Of course, the officer may wisely summon one or more additional officers before even making an approach. Concurrently, the officer can talk to the occupants by using the police car's outside loud speaker system. Explanations or instructions may be given as support personnel are on the way, thus buying time.

If the occupants are suspected of more than a mere traffic violation, it is wise to treat the approach in line with tactics used for a felony stop on any vehicle. This calls for additional officers in more cars and the positioning of officers and units so as to weaken the will of the suspects to resist. Of course, police must be mindful of fields of fire, not just from the occupants but from other officers. Police must also be mindful of safety of citizens, too, including those passing by in other traffic lanes or moving around the vehicles on a road median or shoulder.

In summary, vans, RVs and motor homes are a fact of police life and are here to stay. The occupants of some will be sought for crimes. The hazardous nature of dealing with persons in these kinds of vehicles is well known and police must take thoughtful measures to minimize risks in the course of stopping and approaching under these conditions.

CHAPTER VII

LEGISLATIVE COUNTERMEASURES

CRIME CONTROL seems very closely linked with the prompt reporting of offenses, the early detection of offenders, their immediate arrest and speedy trial, their conviction and realistic sentencing. These are the elements of deterrence, causing suspects to sense the certainty that something will happen, and soon, if they misbehave. Officer safety seems inextricably linked to these steps.

Legislative bodies are supposed to be responsive to public pressure and reflect society's attitude on issues. Sometimes it works this way and sometimes it doesn't. In any event, these bodies can help make police safer if they take favorable action on certain measures. Specific proposals about stiffening gun laws, making capital punishment a reality rather than a hollow folly, and mandating that there be an autopsy whenever an officer is murdered would be sensible to enact into law. So would measures concerning license plates and the use of solar glass in cars. These laws indirectly affect police officer safety.

Legislative bodies do not always act favorably on measures which relate to officer safety. For example, the prospect that the United States Congress might make attacks on police, firemen and judicial officers a federal offense was at one time in the offing. But hearings held in 1970 before the United States Senate's Subcommittee to Investigate the Administration of the Internal Security Act and Other Internal Security Laws, a subcommittee of the Senate's Committee on the Judiciary, proved inconclusive. Evidence presented before the subcommittee was not sufficiently persuasive to cause the United States Senate to pass a bill in this sector. Nevertheless, Congress may again consider whether felonious attacks on these public employees should be a federal offense with investigative responsibility shared by the state and the Federal Bureau of Investigation. A similar statute exists with the National Bank

113

Robbery Act and the respective states' robbery statutes. This is an intricate issue which needs airing and analyses, given today's street action. If passed, such an act may be helpful to reducing attacks on officers.

On the other hand, in 1974 the U.S. Congress passed a measure which was introduced to help streamline the criminal justice system. The act sought to process accused criminals more quickly and efficiently without impairing their constitutional rights. This was the federal Speedy Trial Act which called for a gradual reduction in the time between arrest and trial, the time span narrowing each year over the four years to July 1, 1979. The consequence was that if a defendant is not brought to trial within the specified time, his attorney may move to have the charges dismissed. About 40 states have embraced versions of the Speedy Trial Act.

Speedy trial acts are believed to help make police safer because they take delay out of the system and set a get-to-trial time limit for all felony cases, including trials for those suspects who are free on bail and those who have murdered police. Such legislation has, among other virtues, the benefit of taking delay from the arsenal of defense attorneys, who sometimes use the tactic to their client's advantage.

FIREARMS CONTROL LEGISLATION

Firearms control legislation is hardly ever out of sight. It seems to regularly resurface after the shooting of a prominent American. It surely is among the most contentious, hotly debated and emotional of America's domestic public safety issues. It is also one of the most misunderstood.

Public opinion polls consistently indicate that over two of every three Americans feel there should be tighter legislative reins over hand gun sales and that it be mandatory to register handguns. Yet when such legislation pends in either state house or before the United States Congress, most mail comes from those who feel otherwise. Public opinion and mail lobbyists all agree that steps should be taken to curb crime. But the people disagree, and often heatedly, on the question of whether a crackdown on gun sales and the implementation of comprehensive gun registration would be an effective deterrent.

The all-time leading American spokesman for rigid firearms control legislation was J. Edgar Hoover. Consistently and unstintingly, he

touted the most stringent controls. In September, 1967 he wrote point-
edly in **The FBI Law Enforcement Bulletin** that:

> "There is no doubt in my mind that the easy accessibility of firearms
> is responsible for many killings, both impulse and premeditated. The
> statistics are grim and realistic. Strong measures must be taken, and
> promptly, to protect the public."

Hoover called firearms seven times more lethal than other murder
weapons. His point is underscored by the fact that of the 2,129 lawmen
murdered from 1960-1984, 2,014 (or 94.6 percent) were victims of firearms. Handguns, in contrast to long guns, took 1,506 (or 70.7 percent)
of the 2,129 officers' lives.

The correlation between the ready availability of handguns and assaults and murders of police officers should be of urgent interest to
authorities. There is a strong indication that one of the really meaningful long-range measures which the United States Congress could take to
reduce assaults on police, is the passage of effective federal handgun
controls. Ideally, the stiff measures should be implemented by the states
as well.

Historically, the first instance of state regulation of the purchase and
possession of firearms is found in the controversial Sullivan Law in New
York State, enacted in 1911. The traditional objection raised to this type
of regulation is the usual one against all firearm legislation: it burdens
the law-abiding citizen and fails to keep the pistol out of the hands of the
criminal who will not obey the law but who will steal, bootleg, or even
make a firearm. Proponents of this form of gun control do not deny this.
In fact, one benefit to be derived from a stiff Sullivan-type law is that it
provides a basis for easily convicting gun-carrying criminals. This is
true even where there is insufficient evidence to prove guilt beyond a
reasonable doubt for a major offense such as murder, aggravated assault
or robbery. Proving that a gunman merely possessed a firearm without a
license is simple compared with proving that he participated in a major
crime. If the sentences for possessing unlicensed firearms were stiff, **and**
the judiciary applied them consistently and with vigor, perhaps fewer
suspects would go about their crimes while routinely armed.

Gun registration is not to be confused with gun confiscation, though
it frequently is misunderstood as such. Registration is merely a matter
of recording to whom each firearm rightfully belongs and thus establishing accountability, as has been done for decades with automobiles. To
suggest that registering firearms, certainly all handguns, equates with or
will lead to confiscation is completely illogical. It would be like declaring

that a law to keep unsafe cars off city streets will result in the confiscation of all autos. But as long as easily concealable handguns continue to exact their lethal toll of police, departments should take strong stands supporting handgun registration.

In the long run, it is apparent to many groups that stricter gun control measures, including handgun registration, are needed. Handgun registration infringes on no one's right to keep and bear arms. It might, however, sharply reduce a potential officer killer's ability to murder. Registration may in and of itself prove to be insufficient, too. But waiting for the day when the nation's political leaders realize that handguns are killing more Americans than they are protecting, it stands as a stopgap measure until more control is exerted on the unlawful use of firearms.

Almost every major advisory commission on crime since 1966 has advocated strong firearms control measures as one way to make life in the United States safer. None indicated that legislation, if adopted, would bring about a change in the firearms picture overnight. Rather, measures along these lines, of the kind that Director Hoover ardently supported during his lifetime, are really long-range in impact, benefiting our grandchildren.

The staggering percentage of criminal homicides perpetrated against police by firearms suggest that some kind of gun restraint is warranted. It certainly is overdue as applies to handguns, leaving long guns out of the issue. But the only recent legislative success on the national level to restrict guns has been the passage of the firearms provisions of the Omnibus Crime Control and Safe Streets Act and the Gun Control Act of 1968. This was the first important federal effort to curb the proliferation of weapons in America since 1934 when the National Firearms Act imposed a ban on ownership of the submachine guns that were widely used in organized-crime gang wars of the time.

Although widely balleyhooed at the time of passage, the 1968 legislative provisions merely slowed the booming mail-order gun business through which Lee Harvey Oswald bought the Italian army surplus rifle used to murder President John F. Kennedy. Yet a loophole in the legislation, intended to curb the massive trade in cheap pistols called "Saturday night specials," allowed import of parts for these specials, but not the completed pistol. So parts were imported and the cheap handguns were assembled domestically. In fact, during the four years since the new gun control laws became effective—1969 through 1972—imports of parts for cheap, pot metal street guns were sufficient to see the production of more than 4 million "Saturday night specials."

There has been maxi-rhetoric but mini-legislation on the gun control scene since 1968. A major disappointment hit police in 1984 when a bill to ban armor-piercing ammunition which had been ricocheting around Congress for several years was still unpassed. That year the cop killer bullet bill was lobbied to death by gun interests, fearing that if such a measure succeeded it may be but a prologue to significant firearms control legislation. If passed, the measure would have banned the manufacture, importation and sale of armor-piercing bullets. The bill is certain to be introduced again. Hopefully, the solons will score a hit rather than another near miss of the earlier years.

The handgun debate goes on and on. In the meantime, the most realistic short-term solution appears to be for local police to strictly enforce registration and licensing prerequisites before handgun or rifle purchase. Another helpful measure would be for states that have not yet done so to pass mandatory prison sentencing laws for conviction of serious crimes, including those in which the use of firearms, real or simulated, played a prominent role. This suggests that laws be passed which would call for specific terms in prison without parole for persons convicted of using or simulating a handgun in the course of a crime. The mandatory minimum sentences may be longer if persons were convicted of a gun-use case after a previous conviction for a similar or other violent crime.

In conclusion, there is irony in the gun control squabble of a sadly humorous sort. President Reagan does not like federal handgun legislation. In 1983 he told this to a group of 4,000 National Rifle Association members, to their delight. The irony is that those who attended that speech had to walk past metal detectors to hear the President, himself once a victim of a violent attack involving a handgun, excoriate gun control!

CAPITAL PUNISHMENT

Since the 1972 United States Supreme Court's **Furman vs. Georgia** decision, several states and the federal government have made capital punishment mandatory for specific classes of offenses.[1] By passing such

---

[1]408 U.S. 238, 92 S. Ct. 2726, 22 L.Ed.2d 346 (1972).

legislation, the states have attempted to draft around the question of whether capital punishment **per se** constitutes cruel and unusual punishment.

The alleged merits of capital punishment are linked with several familiar arguments: it acts as a deterrent to murder; prevents future heinous crimes from being committed; and serves the retributive side of justice. Add to this the fact that when kidnapping had reached epidemic proportion in the mid-1930s and was made punishable by death, the act disappeared almost at once. It is also argued that the number of murders across America would go down if the number of legal executions went up—if a death sentence in fact meant death. These considerations, be they real or imagined, weigh heavily on the mind of police officers. Capital punishment also seems to serve police as a morale booster. Indeed, many officers feel their lives endangered if capital punishment is eliminated by judicial fiat. Officers also feel their lives to be endangered if states that have capital punishment are in fact not executing condemned killers.

Whether the arguments propounded for capital punishment are scientifically valid or not is another matter. It needs to be recognized, regardless of how little proof is available for retention of capital punishment, that law enforcement personnel favor it highly. Analyzing the subtleties of intent in the mind of a cop-killer is a difficult task. It is hard to say that an officer's life could have been saved had capital punishment been in effect at the time of an incident. No one, other than the suspect himself, really knows for sure whether the threat of execution would have averted his action.

One offshoot of capital punishment may work against its real or imagined deterrent value. It seems that capital punishment prolongs court proceedings because of the certainty that if convicted, the condemned person will pursue every avenue of appeal available to reverse the death sentence. In Oklahoma, as in most other states, death sentence convictions are automatically referred to the Court of Criminal Appeals for review, a process which up to 1985 took five or more years in several instances.

Another offshoot is the prospect that if punishments are so severe, juries will be reluctant to impose them. The added weight that the question of life or death imposes on jury deliberations sometimes prompts acquittals or findings of a less severe degree of murder. This spirit may have been at work in Oklahoma. For example, of the 69 suspects in the

52 Oklahoma police murder incidents only two were actually executed, although seven sentences of death were handed down.

If these contentions are true in death-penalty states, then these are strong considerations to be analyzed in the debate over capital punishment. If punishment is uncertain, even with the death penalty on the books, the deterrent effect seems compromised.

Arguments whirl, pro and con, about capital punishment, yet morale and deterrent effect are the major factors which police officers see as favoring capital punishment. It follows that as long as police are fired upon and officers continue to be murdered in the line of duty, these two factors should be acknowledged as substantial rationale as legislators reach their decision.

There is still considerable uncertainty about whether capital punishment is fact or folklore in many of the 38 states which, in mid-1985, had death penalty laws. In fact, from 1976 to mid-1985 only some 45 men and one woman have been executed from among the 1,500 prisoners on death rows nationwide. Florida, Louisiana, Georgia and Texas have accounted for all but about 12 of the executions.

In conclusion, here are some interesting figures. Over the ten years, 1975-1984, there were 204,000 homicide victims in America. During this same time only 32 persons were executed, an average of but one murderer for every 6,375 victims. Since 1984 the pace of executions has quickened across America, though it has not become a groundswell. It has come at a time when public support for carrying out the death penalty hovers at about the 67 percent approval mark, virtually a 30-year high. Police officers hope the time will soon come when executions are no longer front-page news, for they will see that as justice served.

AUTOPSY LEGISLATION

An autopsy, a post-mortem medical examination of a body, can also be classified as a countermeasure. Its value is that a qualified pathologist and staff can establish a person's cause of death through standard medical practices. The facts will not only help an investigation and prosecution, but are invaluable for future research into police deaths. Mandating that there must be an autopsy every time a police officer is killed in the line of duty would help assure a complete accounting of what happened.

During the Oklahoma police murders research project the official autopsy report in one case began, "The body is that of an adult, unembalmed white male that measures 191 cm., (75″) in length, and weighs approximately 80 kgs., (175 lbs.). The body is naked. There is complete rigor mortis and the body temperature is cool." The officer was, the report went on, ". . . the victim of a gunfire incident which occurred . . . during application of a District Court Search Warrant for narcotics and dangerous drugs at the described residence."

As unemotional, clinical, precise and scientific as the autopsy report may be, the importance of it in this case was found in the last entry. That entry, labeled "Final Impression of the Cause of Death," provided the district attorney with the basis for convicting the suspect in this incident. The state, backed by medical facts, could set out the specific cause of death, leaving that fact virtually immune from defense inferences that death may not have been actually perpetrated by the defendant.

Autopsy surgery is one of the oldest procedures in medical science. Its purpose is to meet the need for detailed diagnosis of the cause of death. Moreover, it is important since as many as one-fourth of the determinations of cause of death made at the scene by physicians and police may be inaccurate. Clearly, there is a reason for performing an autopsy and it is not idle medical curiosity as many people believe.

Adequate medico-legal investigation is absolutely essential to law enforcement and the prosecution of crime. It answers such crucial questions as: (1) what was the exact cause of death; (2) was death caused by one, two or more gunshot wounds, etc., a blunt instrument, asphyxiation, or a fall; and (3) was the obvious wound really the cause of death? Other urgent questions, too, should be resolved by autopsy when a police officer is an apparent murder victim, for the case may become entangled in a hotly contested trial. Also, an analysis of post mortem findings may help police training officers point to other preventive measures that can be taken to further protect officers from homicidal assaults.

The state medical examiner system, under which autopsies may be conducted, is the modern equivalent of a creaking, antiquated coroner system. The coroner system was developed by English knights who served the Crown hundreds of years ago. A modern state medical examiner law requires all deaths known or suspected to have resulted from accident, suicide or homicide to be subject to the jurisdiction of the state medical examiner, a qualified pathologist. This is true regardless of the period of survival following the injury and whether there was medical attendance during time of the survival.

In Oklahoma such a law has been in effect since 1962. From 1910 through 1961 state law called for justices of the peace to perform the functions of the coroner. There was no requirement that justices or coroner's jury members possess medical knowledge or investigative skills. Moreover, justices of the peace serving as coroners were not required to hold inquests in every case of violent death. Discretion in such matters was a characteristic of the system.

Fortunately, autopsy is becoming a normal procedure when lawmen are murdered in Oklahoma, a product of the medical examiner's law. Moreover, that there are usually autopsies even in remote areas of the state where facilitates for autopsy are less than ideal, is evidence that the medical examiner law is working.

In conclusion, the rapidly changing character of American society adds a new urgency to the importance of a detailed post mortem medical diagnosis. Moreover, the importance of competent medico-legal investigations of death is not linked merely to trial testimony. It is necessary to take the speculation out of cause of death in an era of national violence and suspicion of government and its agents. The procedure is essential to the resolution of civil suits, especially those which may be linked with litigation over worker's compensation and life insurance settlements. It is especially relevant where double indemnity payment may be an issue!

MANDATING LICENSE PLATE IMPROVEMENTS

Virtually all traffic stops which police make for hazardous moving violations involve approaching the vehicle and driver from the rear. Also, the procedure in almost all forces calls for the arresting officer to radio notice of the car's make and license number to the dispatch center. There, routinely, a check is made against the stolen car list. Ideally, this entire procedure occurs before the officer leaves the patrol car to contact the suspect driver.

Reasons other than traffic stops might make it necessary for officers to interview persons in autos or to approach unoccupied cars. There are occasions when police approach cars which appear disabled or abandoned; when persons in autos appear intoxicated, unruly, sick, or asleep; and instances where the occupants seem to be acting furtively, as if concealing some suspicious activity. Sometimes an officer's intuition tells him that occupants warrant a routine check. Officers often must make their approach from in front of the auto, or from an angle, as from a sidewalk.

When making a non-traffic vehicle approach, an officer should check the license plate against the hot sheet before committing himself. It is desirable in some circumstances that the dispatcher be advised, just as when a traffic stop is made. There are additional reasons. The front reflectorized license plate helps officers to see parked vehicles at night, too. Also, most police patrolling is on two-way streets, much of which is in cities and towns when an officer will see many more front than rear plates because he is constantly closing on oncoming vehicles. Another reason for mandating front and rear automobile license plates is that during heavy winter blizzards the snow is likely to cover the rear plate, leaving only the front plate as a means of vehicle identification.

A compelling reason is that front and rear reflectorized plates would enable more accurate identification of vehicles suspected of being driven by drivers impaired by alcohol or other drugs.

In 1985, there were 20 states as well as Guam, the Mariana Islands and Puerto Rico which issued but one passenger car license plate, rather than two, to be mounted on the rear of the vehicle. These states are: Alabama, Arkansas, Connecticut, Delaware, Florida, Georgia, Indiana, Kansas, Kentucky, Louisiana, Massachusetts, Michigan, Mississippi, New Mexico, North Carolina, Oklahoma, Pennsylvania, South Carolina, Tennessee and West Virginia. The absence of a front plate on cars registered in these states and outlying areas places an officer at a sharp initial disadvantage. It denies him the opportunity to check the plate against the stolen list when making an angle or frontal approach. Moreover, in 1985 there were still four states and Puerto Rico and the Virgin Islands whose passenger car license plates were not reflectorized to ease night identification. These states are Kentucky, Maryland, Michigan, and New Jersey.

All 13 Canadian provinces and territories also should mandate that there be reflectorized license plates on the front and rear of each passenger vehicle. In 1985 all Canadian territories and provinces except Alberta, Prince Edward Island and Quebec mandated two plates per car. The reflectorization picture was far less satisfactory: the provinces of Newfoundland and Labrador, Ontario, Prince Edward Island and the Yukon and Northwest Territories had opted against this helpful measure.

That assaults and officer injuries could have been prevented if there had been a front or reflectorized plate on a suspect car is speculative. However, all indications suggest that there were several instances when officers were victimized for want of a front plate for early identification.

It is timely for these states and Canadian provinces to pass legislation requiring that each vehicle bear front and rear reflectorized license plates. This is a small, inexpensive countermeasure that can mean a great deal to the safety of officers on patrol as well as aiding them in the performance of their duties. The actual cost of a pair of reflectorized license plates to a state is very nominal—about $1.00 a set—and may easily, and properly, be passed on to the motoring public. Small cost when compared with the toll in officer injuries and fatalities.

NONTRANSPARENT OR REFLECTIVE GLASS

Modern technology has fostered many innovations to ease life and enhance comfort. Within the past few years one product—nontransparent or highly solar reflective glass—has been used in the construction industry to enhance building appearance and reduce air conditioning costs. Now the product has been adapted for installation as motor vehicle glass. Used as auto glass, the cab becomes reflective and nontransparent when viewed from the outside.

Police officers handle millions of cases a year involving motor vehicles. An officer's inability to readily see inside or through extremely darkly tinted windows under normal day or lighted conditions, constitutes a grave danger to him. So do full-window picture decals by dramatically reducing visibility from outside in, placing officers at a distinct disadvantage, too. A few states have passed legislation to prevent the use of super solar material and full picture decals in a motor vehicle. More states should follow. Officers would be grateful.

CHAPTER VIII

STILL OTHER COUNTERMEASURES

THERE ARE still other casualty reduction possibilities which exceed proposals set out earlier. Their shaping and further development will help departments and individuals cope, long and short range, with the immensely complicated problem of attacks on police.

One of the most immediate measures that forces can take is to make certain that the public is informed about the dangers facing their police. Additionally, police forces should frankly confront the problems which alcohol and other drugs pose for officers, as well as the impact of television and movie violence on street cops. While not a casualty reduction measure as such, police should seek to see that benefits afforded survivors are adequate in the event a life is lost.

Programs which follow might make positive contributions and ought to be thoroughly examined by appropriate persons, bodies and agencies.

INFORMING THE PUBLIC OF THE
DANGERS FACING POLICE

American police officers are a key form of institutional authority. Lawmen bear burdensome and important responsibilities, duties, powers, and prerogatives as society's enforcers of the law. They are the living embodiment of liberty within a framework of order. Yet the police, as the most visible symbols of government, have come under sharp philosophical and personal attack in the past 25 years. That physical assaults on police have occurred in alarming numbers and intensity during this span is shown in Table 1 on page xiv. The data confirm that attacks remain a serious concern and of considerable magnitude to the victims—police officers. They need public support **now**, more than ever.

"Support Your Local Police" is a phrase which can lead to more than support. If citizen energies are properly channeled, police lives may be saved. Citizen support for police is by no means a novel concept. Yet the public must know what can be most useful, and then be encouraged to act.

Spreading information is vital, once the force has agreed to what it would like citizens to do to help. Community service officers and uniformed members, especially, should be well versed in the public involvement game plan. Moreover, all civilian and sworn police personnel must know the "hows" and "whys" of police work and excel in describing their work and needs to the public. The more citizens understand about the work of police, the easier it will be for the public to assist officers.

The police, themselves, must know about non-police programs which, if used by the public, can help officers, too. For example, after a large western city established a mental health care center as one of its social service activities, the police department distributed a one-page bulletin to all officers explaining the center's role and services and who was entitled to use them. Officers were then able to spread the word to the people on the street. The citizens become aware that the mental health clinic could help them face their problems. Quite possibly, this information may have prevented family disturbances or other related stress situations. This helps police.

DEALING WITH ALCOHOL

Except as applies to alcohol consumption and drunken driving, Americans have yet to be brought to their senses about the impact of excessive drinking on violence and death. Other than combatting officer carelessness and complacency, there is no single front where a breakthrough could prove more meaningful to saving people from trauma than to successfully deal with alcohol. The problem is immense, touching almost every area of life, yet is shrugged off. Raw figures are sobering but all too often are cast aside as applying to "the other guy" who is the culprit.

The nation's Number One mental health problem begs for public understanding and a national commitment to resolution. Voices heralding the issue seem drowned out by other causes, for few want to tangle with the bottled phantom which affects most of us so immediately and so embarrassingly.

Tippling, as portrayed by night club comics, in movies and on commercial television, loses its humor when the casualty list stemming from alcohol consumption is featured. By any measuring stick, alcohol is an enormous problem of millions of Americans. There is practically no household which doesn't suffer its impact very directly one way or another each year.

How? Because, according to the United States Department of Health, Education and Welfare and the Congressional Office of Technology Assessment there are:

1. Some 95 million Americans who drink alcoholic beverages, of whom about one in every ten either is an alcoholic (being physically dependent on alcohol) or is an alcohol abuser, a person who drinks to excess;

2. Some 28,000 fatalities from auto crashes each year where alcohol was a factor;

3. Figures showing about one of every two persons who commit homicides consumed alcohol before the crime;

4. Over 137 billion dollars lost to U.S. industry each year because of alcohol abuse;

5. Greater incidence of alcoholism among American Indians, about twice the national average; and

6. Unfortunate indications that excessive drinking is a response among minority group members to such hardships as blocked opportunities, inadequate medical care, unemployment, poor housing and schooling, and so forth.

Alcohol is America's most abused drug and at the same time the most advertised and misrepresented. It is consistently presented by giant commercial enterprises as encouraging humor and assuring conviviality and popularity among people. By clever nuances, advertising suggests that alcohol opens one's avenues to business success, underscores one's sophistication and maturity, and helps people solve problems. In truth, the alcohol picture mirrors a massive health problem which impacts on police officers enormously in many, many ways.

Officers see no humor, conviviality, maturity, sophistication or problems solved in scenes like this: a teetering armed husband who, drink crazed, has savagely beaten his wife and kids. He holds a firearm, declaring his intention to kill the first officer who attempts to intervene in what he says is "only my business." Madison Avenue whitewashes this picture as they huckster alcoholic beverages.

Drinking by suspects in the Oklahoma study was apparently a salient factor in over one of every two of the 52 officer murder incidents. This parallels the alcohol consumption factor in homicides generally. So any way you look at it, alcohol consumption by suspects poses a giant headache and source of potential trouble for police officers.

No certain, exclusive alcohol countermeasure will suddenly free police from interacting with people who have been drinking. Prohibition didn't work. Liquor laws have proven no solution, and their enforcement is very arbitrary. In fact, if anything has emerged from 60 years of experimentation with this massive social problem, it is that no dramatic changes have been effected among Americans as a group, and problem drinkers specifically.

National failure notwithstanding, there are reasons to try to face the problem squarely and nurture programs which may prove useful.

First, the nation should continue its long-range program to prevent alcohol abuse and alcoholism among young people. Education and the schools are crucial here. Intensification of the program is clearly warranted.

Second, and there is movement along this front, new means must be tried for handling persons who fall into police hands for drunkenness without accompanying criminal misbehavior. The decriminalization of drunkenness may prove beneficial in the long-range as adequately staffed detoxification units and aftercare facilities become reality.

Third, alcoholism warrants treatment as an illness, not a criminal offense, and there is progress toward implementing this concept. The notion that alcohol is America's largest untreated, treatable illness is gaining backers from many quarters, including from professional athletes.

There are other measures possible in combatting alcohol-induced misbehavior. These are set out with the full, if disappointing, realization that physicians, psychologists and psychiatrists have been unable to discover any single treatment method that will invariably produce satisfactory results.

Fourth, the American attitude, that alcohol is essential and must be routinely featured at various fraternal, social and business get-togethers, must be changed.

Fifth, alcohol is a drug and must be identified and understood as such. People must know what they are drinking and that while its consumption can cause a person to feel relaxed and at ease, it can also lower inhibitions, slow normal response times and encourage aggression and foolishness. In short, the societal use of alcohol obliges a person to accept accompanying responsibilities of a very grave personal nature.

Sixth, there must be greater respect afforded those who either do not use or do not abuse alcohol. Persons must understand that their conduct, including their use or nonuse of alcohol, influences people nearby, and also serves as a model for others, especially the young and aspiring.

Another measure involves action the police themselves may take. While the alcohol factor is high as pertains to suspects involved in murders of officers, if officers themselves who have blossoming alcohol problems can be helped, they may better cope with street problems without the disadvantage of fatigue, mental stress or frayed tempers owing to alcohol debilitation. Police departments, and especially those of more than 100 personnel, must make concerted efforts to identify and treat their problem drinkers. These employed near-alcoholics are personnel whose alcoholic consumption interferes with efficiency or individual capabilities to a noticeable level. Remedial programs to help these employees may be established through county or state mental health officials. Their mission is to identify the problem drinker, help the person recognize the problem and make suitable referrals for assessment and treatment. This should be done, happily, while the officer is on the job. Larger forces may form Alcoholics Anonymous chapters for their own members along with force-wide education and counseling programs.

Large police departments could model their remedial programs after the Employee Assistance Program (EAP) started in 1973 by corporate giant ITT. This program features a hotline to direct people to treatment, counseling, self-help groups, volunteer agencies, etc. Confidentiality, a program hallmark, means no one must worry about information getting on an employee's personnel record. The program is an important fringe benefit to be utilized by all employees any time they need help, for whatever reason.

In summary, putting a lid on alcohol abuse can help reduce violent crime. No one who has studied history and understands human nature would argue that human beings can be made temperate by repressive measures and legislation alone. Moreover, prohibition has proven a dismal failure. The nation must try a combination of measures — programs, education, legislation, and counseling to name a few. The government's role is not just to underwrite programs set out above but also to advertise the virtues of alcohol restraint, as has been done on a modest basis. The government's anti-smoking campaign is a good example. The schools can play a prominent role, too, through gutsy education and public health programs. And there must be continuing, concerted research on the social, legal and medical fronts as pertains to alcohol abuse and societal responsibilities.

TELEVISION AND MOVIE VIOLENCE

What a paradox! People pack theaters to see films featuring violence at its worst, coldly and explicitly done. Then they head home to communities where crime rates are spiraling. Meanwhile, those too fearful to go out at night turn on television at home and settle in to enjoy the evening's ripoffs, fighting, shooting and murder, safe behind deadbolted doors. In short, it's hard to find an evening of commercial or cable media free from heavy violence, often of a very explicit sort.

Television and movie violence probably triggers far more violence against police than will ever be documented. Often copfighting is made to appear the norm, an acceptable, usual part of every police-suspect transaction. It has almost reached the point where any two-bit hoodlum feels compelled to fight, rather than to surrender peacefully, as many used to do. Waging a titanic fight for all to see, just like his fictional counterparts in common police thrillers do, gives him identity among his pals. Police face great uncertainty as to how the action will go down when making arrests. This is especially true if suspects must be taken from among their friends or out of crowded public places. The influence of the media may be one reason.

Some people say that violence is a fact of life and inherent in the nature of humans. These people see violence as an art form and favor depicting it as such. But need it be portrayed so precisely and so graphically? Such violence may titillate the most latent desires of emotionally strained people who need only the blueprint for violence to induce them to act.

To no one's surprise, violence on television has been shown to encourage violence on the streets. This was one of the conclusions of the 1968 National Commission on the Causes and Prevention of Violence. It was reconfirmed in 1982 by a National Institute of Mental Health study which flatly stated that it found overwhelming evidence that excessive violence on television causes aggressive behavior in children.

The problem has not eased, especially among youths from broken and poor families. These kids, and even those better off economically but lacking relationships of depth or meaning, often play out roles suggested by television as substitutes for real-life experiences. Without realizing it, kids fall prey to the fact that a television set is a stage in everyone's living room and where fantasy is presented without a satisfactory demarkation line between reality and make-believe. Small wonder that some teenagers use violence as a means for being recognized and establishing their own identity. For them, violence is the pathway to big-shotism, as well as for kicks.

The specific cause-and-effect relationship between movie and television violence and actual crime is yet to be irrefutably set out. It's a highly contentious issue with a host of social variables being drawn into the hassle. In our nation the big-stakes political winners need to come across well on television. They know that television is a big league communications device with great impact on public opinion. Moreover, nothing draws a crowd around the television set quicker than roughhouse ice hockey or a brawl on the football field. Noted roughhouse professional athletes, ironically called policemen in ice hockey, have not only become rich; they have carved out a unique niche for themselves and created a subtle mystique about violence. The visual media—especially television, but also movies—is capable of such immense influence on human behavior and personalities that it is naive to discount its influence on criminal behavior.

Measures to counter the incessant diet of excessive violence and gory escapist daydreams characterizing some movies and television shows are not easy to set out. Ideally, of course, viewers could turn off over-violent shows or stay away from the box office. Sponsors, too, could help by refusing to underwrite violent programs. Unfortunately, violence and the box office constitute such a profitable commercial union that sponsors are always available. The Federal Communications Commission has made no concerted effort of a sustained sort to root out excessive television violence. Perhaps some controls could be devised and made effective if the FCC took a more vigorous interest in violence and program scheduling. This interest could play a part in its periodic station license renewal examinations.

More can be done by the movie moguls and television tycoons. Self-restraint and professionalism are keys to better stories, ones with greater substance and social messages. Greater concern for what is shown and how it is depicted is the challenge, too, although mercenary interests will balk at taming the violence because their principal yardstick is box office ratings, not social responsibility and taste.

Finally, the police deal with the unsolicited, violent by-products of the visual media. They need relief from it and should clamor for it. If there is progress on no other front, the police themselves may be compelled to act. Through employee organizations, they may spearhead national economic sanctions against sponsors who allow producers to overdo anti-police violence in their shows.

SURVIVOR BENEFITS

The most significant survivor benefit measure ever passed at the federal level of government was the Public Safety Officer Benefits Act of 1976. This measure was initially proposed in 1971 to provide $50,000 to survivors of police officers murdered in the line of duty, irrespective of what level of government they served. It took five years and a host of versions before an act of such high merit was passed by the United States Congress. The law is regularly being fine-tuned so that deaths attributable to stress or exertion encountered in the course of duty will fall under the act's umbrella.

In spite of the significant congressional action, other aspects of survivors benefits must be evaluated and, if appropriate, remedial action taken to ameliorate problems. For example, in some places officers rendering assistance to nearby jurisdictions may lose their eligibility for local benefits by merely crossing their own city or county lines. Also, smaller communities often lack the financial resources to provide a reasonable level of service-connected death, injury and illness benefits.

Clearly, the need is **now** for meaningful survivor benefits legislation to be passed by state governments to supplement the federal measure. Ideally, benefit packages the states may pass should include medical care, compensation for temporary, total, and permanent disability and monthly compensation for an officer's survivors.

In at least 58 places across America, public spirited citizens have formed associations to provide some financial security for survivors of officers killed in the line of duty. These groups, called Hundred Clubs, were organized in Detroit in 1952 following the murder of an officer there. Hundred Clubs cannot fill the financial gap between a survivor's dollar needs and benefits which inure to him or her through the spouse's employer, but the organization tries to ease the burden by making a lump sum payment to help with immediate and near-range expenses. Hundred Clubs representatives have lobbied and ardently in favor of death benefits legislation.[2]

While not a preventive measure, a survivor benefits program would provide officers a sense of security, knowing that if they are murdered their families have financial help, at least for a few years. Lump sum payments legislation is a significant beginning, but more could be made to happen. The United States Congress could also consider enacting a national life insurance program to cover all public employees slain in the line of duty, including police, firefighters and correctional personnel. The program could be broadened to include compensation for line-of-duty injury or incapacitation stemming from assaults, too.

While neither a countermeasure nor legislative proposal as such, a police force owes the family of an officer who is fatally injured in the line of duty help of a special sort. That is, assistance of varying kinds for the widow (or widower) about the problems to be faced as a survivor. There are predictable legal and technical problems which will come suddenly into the life of a surviving mate. Some of these entanglements are very complicated; all are very emotional and come at a time when survivors may not be thinking clearly.

While line of duty death will touch only a few households, the eventualities should be frankly anticipated by every police family. Young police couples should not postpone deciding what arrangement should be made in the event of death. Also, senior couples must be certain that arrangements made earlier are still timely. Moreover, it is urgent that important personal records are kept and are readily accessible, such as insurance papers, birth and marriage certificates and financial and banking papers and wills. Wills must not only be in order, but updated and accessible, too. Custodian accounts, pension board and social security information, fringe benefit agreements, veterans' benefits, police association or union records and so forth are important documents which need to be updated frequently. Income tax records and any contracts and school transcripts should also be at hand. Safety deposit box keys, the number and combination of the officer's departmental locker and keys to any other equipment repositories or offices must be available, too.

---

[2]Ordway P. Burden is President of the Law Enforcement Assistance Foundation, Inc., and is a Hundred Club founder. He may be reached at 651 Colonial Blvd., Washington Township, Westwood P.O., New Jersey 07675. Phone: 201-666-4400.

Finally, it would be very helpful if the department made a competent financial advisor available to the survivor at this troubled time. This person's services may be provided as a benefit of union or police association membership or perhaps through the jurisdiction's personnel department. The force should urge officers to maintain never-ending orderliness in their personal affairs. At the minimum, the parent police force should assist the survivor with initiating the following steps:

1. Notify the deceased's retirement system.
2. Contact the local social security office to determine eligibility for any death or survivor benefits.
3. Initiate steps which will lead to benefits stemming from the Public Safety Officer Benefits Act of 1976.
4. If applicable, notify the veterans' administration and other organizations regarding death benefits.
5. Notify the family lawyer and all insurance agents.
6. Notify the bank and other firms where the deceased had accounts, debts or loans.
7. Obtain the needed number of certified copies of the death certificate from the funeral home.
8. Obtain the original copy of the will and of all stocks, bonds, savings certificates, passbooks, ownership deeds, etc., so that an inventory may be made for estate purposes.
9. File an income tax return on the deceased's behalf.
10. Help the survivors make contact with appropriate support groups.

CHAPTER IX

A FERTILE SECTOR FOR
RESEARCH

AS THE President's Commission on Law Enforcement and Administration of Justice so aptly observed, ". . . the greatest need is the need to know . . ." much more about the American justice system. Research, the key to knowing much more about all sorts of things, is sorely needed in order to get a better handle on the anatomy of attacks on police. Surprisingly little research has been done in this specific sector in spite of the epidemic nature of assaults on police.

Since 1960 the most widely used information about the assault and murder of police has been the annual statistics provided by the Federal Bureau of Investigation, shown in Table 1. Though useful because they give a sense of how extensive the problem of cop fighting is, the FBI data are merely numbers which are limited in scope and are under-reported. Moreover, they lack analyses and have never adequately addressed the specific questions pertaining to murders and assaults which must be researched in any thorough study of violence against law enforcement officers.

Over the years many reports about cop fighting have been written by law enforcement officials or journalists and published in news magazines. These are highly impressionistic reports generally based on day-to-day observations by a police officer or an investigative writer and are not research. They focus on specific operational aspects of attacks on police and provided no systematic treatment of the many factors surrounding assault and murder incidents. Impressionistic essays continue to be published but they show little that's new in their perceptiveness and analyses, although all underscore the vexing problem of cop fighting and police murders.

Despite the urgency of the assault and murder problem, little of a technical and analytical nature was known about assaults on police and their murders until mid-1974. At that time a report stemming from a 20-month study on the subject, under sponsorship of a grant from the U.S. Department of Justice, was published by the University of Oklahoma.[1] This research subjected violence against police to a deliberate, broadly-based and systematic analysis. The project, called The Police Assaults Study, had as its data base information assembled over calendar year 1973 from 37 municipal law enforcement agencies in the five southwestern states. These totaled well over 1,100 accounts of assaults on officers ranging from encounters where no injuries were suffered to those resulting in the murder of police. From these the research team compiled a descriptive profile of assaults with three main categories of information: (1) officer characteristics; (2) assailant characteristics; and (3) the assault itself. Under officer characteristics, the analysis of height, build, race, rank, age, length of service and training yielded little to indicate that any particular kind of police officer is more liable than others to be attacked. The traditional belief that "little" policemen attract more trouble than "big" ones was not borne out by the data.

Assailant characteristics also indicated that short people, although represented among assailants, are not more likely to assault police officers than taller ones. Women were less likely to commit assaults than men. Nonwhites were not more likely to assault police than whites. The average age of assailants was 28.2 years; the under-18's represented an amazingly low percentage. Unemployed persons were more likely to commit assaults than people in a job. Persons of lower socio-economic status constituted a disproportionately large percentage. Alcohol was identified as a highly salient factor among those attacking officers.

The assault incident itself, about which complex data were assembled, yielded useful information: The majority of assaults occurred during the hours of darkness, the leisure and drinking hours. The greatest frequency was during July and over one-third took place at the weekend, one quarter on Saturdays. Over one-third were on streets or highways, many coming while an officer was attempting an arrest.

---

[1]This project was supported by the Law Enforcement Assistance Administration under Grant Numbers 73-TA-06-004 and 73-DF-06-0053. A three-volume **Final Report** and an **Operations Research Manual** were published on June 28, 1974 by the Bureau of Government Research at the University of Oklahoma.

The next highest scene was the private residence, confirming that the domestic dispute is a prime setting for assaults on police. Ten percent took place during charging or detention, identifying the jail as a far more hazardous site than most people realize. Officers on auto patrol were by far the most often assaulted. The presence of more than one officer by no means reduced the likelihood of assault for in 87.6 percent of the cases more than one lawman was there. Active physical support by civilian onlookers was given three times as often to police as to assailants but in 60 percent of cases civilian witnesses remained passive or neutral. In over half the assaults the officer was uninjured. In only 2.2 percent of the assaults was a firearm used. These and many more interesting points, with lessons both for operational and training purposes, came out of the police assaults study.

The Oklahoma research staff sub-contracted with the International Association of Chiefs of Police to evaluate the murders of officers stemming from ambush attacks and robberies in progress. The IACP published two risk reduction manuals: **Ambush Attacks** and **Robbery Events.** Both proved to be useful reports which aired means of coping with these vicious attacks on officers primarily by improving police field procedures, equipment and training.

There has not been much more research about attacks on police since the Oklahoma study in spite of the urgent nature of the issue. A few prominent scholars have done some writing but they have not made observations from a project like the police assaults study. On two occasions, **The Annals** of the American Academy of Political and Social Science have highlighted articles about the police and violence.[2] In 1966, an entire issue of **The Annals,** edited by Dr. Thorsten Sellin, included 14 articles dealing with violence. Most of these were concerned with the psychological and sociological aspects of violent behavior. Only one article dealt with aggressive crimes and its writer concluded that the scarcity of statistics prevented identification of trends in this area. None of the 14 articles was precisely on point relative to police officer victimization.

In 1980, **The Annals** filled 156 of its 211-page November issue with 14 more articles, many of which related to the police. Edited by Dr. Lawrence W. Sherman, these covered police against violence; violence against police; and violence by police.

---

[2]Respectively, these are **The Annals** of the American Academy of Political and Social Science, 364 (March, 1966) and 452 (November, 1980).

In this article introducing this issue of **The Annals**, Dr. Sherman acknowledges that little is known about violence against the police:

> "As little as we know about how . . . to reduce civic violence, we know even less about how to reduce violence against the police. The ignorance is surprising given the great official attention and funding the issue has received. . . . Millions of dollars have . . . been spent on supporting the widows, but barely any federal funds have been spent on research to discover how to prevent such deaths. Nor have social scientists . . . initiated much of their own research on violence against the police."

The writers of the 156-page report recognized that while police and violence are central to the American concept of government, there are three questions to answer: (1) how can the police act more effectively and justly against violence in society; (2) how can the violence against police be better understood and then reduced; and (3) what accounts for the wide variation in police use of violence and what can be learned from the variation to reduce police violence to the lowest possible level?

Scholars have raised the questions but unhappily have provided few answers. The **Annals'** conclusion is best summarized by the last paragraph of the 14th article:

> "Shootings are a part of the routine unpredictability of police work. They will occur, but the practical circumstances surrounding their occurrence will vary and therefore so will their meaning. Researchers have sought to code and compare certain features of police shootings such that a descriptive and — ideally — explanatory model or theory can be built . . . it must be remembered that for the police officer such a theory will have no essential application for it will always be superficial to the contextually embedded phenomenon it attempts to understand . . . Though we can never underestimate the potential solace served by a theory, it is, in the end, something that is imposed. Police shootings, as incidents to be studied for the light they cast on various theories of police behavior, will therefore never be clearly understood . . ."

In 1981, Professor David Lester of Stockton State College in New Jersey gave a paper before the Academy of Criminal Justice Sciences. Professor Lester calculated the death rates of police officers murdered from 1971-1978 in the largest American cities and then correlated the data with a host of other crime, suicide, geographical and climatic conditions, city by city. Among other things, he noted that a unique feature of law enforcement as a career is that its personnel have the highest risk of fatality from murder as contrasted to occupational fatality rates from accidental death.

In 1982, three consecutive issues of **The Journal of Police Science and Administration** addressed "Violence and the Police: An Analysis of Robbery-Related Assault Incidents."[3] Dr. James J. Fyfe of the American University notes that Dr. C. Kenneth Meyer, the principal author of the feature, and his colleagues have taken the detailed information about robberies, analyzed it and related the findings to the situations that account for most of the serious injuries and murders of police. Fyfe writes that ". . . they have made a very important contribution to our knowledge about police-citizen violence . . ."

In a 1984 article, David Konstantin found that the majority of incidents in which an officer was murdered was an incident which the officer, rather than a citizen, initiated.[4] He also found that officer deaths stemming from domestic disputes were not so many as is popularly believed, adding that the greatest category of lives lost were while attempting other arrests. Konstantin concluded his feature by declaring that ". . . there exists a real and continuing need for analysis of the killings to . . . effectively address contemporary hazards."

In summary, there is a massive need for research and writing about attacks on police because comparatively little has been done over the years. The subject begs for investigation of an applied sort, with findings being translated into action programs directed toward casualty reduction. This means there must be significant fiscal resources earmarked for research of this nature.

Dollars could be committed to uniquely qualified universities or other agencies to conduct the research. Furthermore, there are governmental units specifically studying violence which could be assigned an appropriate, precise role in such deliberations. One of these is the Violence Epidemiology Branch of the Center for Health Promotion and Education, Centers for Disease Control in Atlanta, Georgia. It may be an appropriate base for research as it does epidemiological research on violence related to rape, homicide, suicide, child abuse, child neglect and spouse abuse but not about attacks on police. Another possible government unit to conduct research about attacks on police is the National Center for the Analysis of Violent Crime (NCAVC),

---

[3]C. Kenneth Meyer, et al, "Violence and the Police: An Analysis of Robbery-Related Assault Incidents," **Journal of Police Science and Administration**, volume 10, numbers 1, 2 and 3 (March, June and September, 1982).

[4]David N. Konstantin, "Homicides of American Law Enforcement Officers, 1978-1980," **Justice Quarterly**, volume 1, number 1 (March, 1984).

headquartered in Quantico, Virginia, at the FBI's National Academy. The NCAVC, developed in 1984, is collecting data about and analyzing serial murders, forcible rapes, arsons and other targeted crimes. In any case, with over a million assaults on officers and 2,129 murdered between 1960-1984, it is timely for either of these relatively new branches of the major U.S. Cabinet-level departments to initiate research about this epidemic.

A third potential base for research about cop killings is the Mental Health branch of the United States Department of Health and Human Services. A fourth prospect, depending upon the level and nature of its funding, is the National Institute of Justice within the U.S. Department of Justice. In addition, there appears to be no valid reason why joint funds from the National Centers for Disease Control and the Mental Health interests could not be parlayed with U.S. Department of Justice funds and used if the scope of research was of sufficient breadth, which it should be. Finally, private foundations should be encouraged to participate, since follow-on research in the area of police casualties is so urgent and the potential pay-off from applied research is so great.

CHAPTER X

CONCLUSION

AMERICAN POLICE officers and policing as an institution will survive the epidemic of attacks on and murders of lawmen and women. Both men and women officers of the system and the system itself have proven resilient, showing impressive will and ability to bounce back. Their character seems aptly described by the words of an old, anonymous Scottish ballad, a tribute to the come-back powers of warriors led by chiefs of courage:

> "Ffight on my men," says Sir Andrew Bartton,
> "I am hurt, but I am not slaine;
> I'le lay me downe and bleed a-while,
> and then I'le rise and ffight againe."

Persistent, prolonged and uncurbed attacks on police could conceivably precipitate unwelcome suppressive countermeasures foreign to a free society. Therefore, it is important that assaults on police be reduced—but within the framework of comprehensive programs which specify carefully reasoned responses. Hopefully, these programs will lessen the number of assaulted police and be evidence of America's commitment to the preservation of life.

In conclusion, while the implementation of various life saving measures is important to reducing casualties, the most critical area is the six inches between the ears of each officer!

INDEX

Compiled by Jeanne G. Howard